# How to

# Win the

# Mortgage

# War

# How to
# Win the
# Mortgage War

## No Mortgage,
## No Debt,
## In as Little as
## Two Years

*David Solomon*

David Solomon

**Sirrom Publishing**
Marlborough, Massachusetts

The following trademarks appear in this book: Saturn, Oldsmobile, Snickers, Milky Way, Craftsman, Bisquick, Heartland, Rolls Royce, VISA, MasterCard, Marriott, First Card, American Airlines, Northwest Airlines, General Motors, Ford, Fab, Kraft, Cracker Barrel, Arnold, All, A1, Pillsbury, Lysol, Tropicana, Grovestand, Edge, Gillette, Sensor, Foamy, Percocet, Xanax, Valium, Pyrex, Brillo, Cub Scouts, Sharp, Carousel II, SensorCook, Better Business Bureau.

"On the House" columns by Carol Hamelin of Century 21 Hamelin, Realtors, Westboro, Massachusetts that appeared in *The Community Advocate*, David Bagdon, Publisher/Editor, Westboro, Massachusetts; "Ernie's House Calls" by Ernie Houde, Realtor, Dallamora Realtors, Marlborough, Massachusetts; and the United States Department of Housing and Urban Development are acknowledged as useful references in preparing Chapters 10-12.

How to Win the Mortgage War
No Mortgage, No Debt, In as Little as Two Years

**Publisher's Cataloging in Publication**
 (*Prepared by Quality Books Inc.*)
 Solomon, David A., 1953-
  How to win the mortgage war : no mortgage, no debt, in as little
 as two years / David Solomon.
   p. cm.
   Includes index.
   Preassigned LCCN: 96-92522
   ISBN 0-9653266-0-8


  1. Mortgages. 2. Finance, Personal.   I. Title.

HG4655.S65 1996              332.72
                             QBI96-40335

**Attention:** Colleges, Universities, Corporations, and Professional Organizations may obtain quantity discounts on bulk purchases of this book for educational, fund raising, or gift-giving purposes. Special booklets or book excerpts can also be created for your specific needs. For more information please contact: Sirrom Publishing, Post Office Box 40, Marlborough, Massachusetts 01752-0040.

# Acknowledgment

My thanks to Kenneth J. Wellington for developing and preparing the tables and figures presented in Chapter 5, Finances 102: Save Many Years and Slash Tens of Thousands of Dollars Off Your Mortgage. Ken's expertise and creativity are evident in his clearly illustrating the financial consequences of mortgages and winning the mortgage war. Ken's many hours of work are greatly appreciated.

The "On the House" columns by Carol Hamelin of Century 21 Hamelin, Realtors, Westboro, Massachusetts that appeared in *The Community Advocate*, David Bagdon, Publisher/Editor, Westboro, Massachusetts; and "Ernie's House Calls" by Ernie Houde, Realtor, Dallamora Realtors, Marlborough, Massachusetts, were useful references in preparing Chapters 10-12.

## To

Morris, Tuckie,
Kathy, Dad, Joanne, and
Carol

# Contents

# Part I

# The Essential Basics

# No Mortgage, No Debt— From Imagination to Reality

Imagine how you will feel free of debt; your home mortgage paid off many years or decades ahead of schedule. Use the strategies and tactics described in this book and enjoy this fantastic feeling. I say that not as a Harvard economist, a Yale accountant, or a millionaire, but as someone who (with my wonderful wife Kathy) achieved and enjoys the debt-free feeling.

You achieve the debt-free feeling over several years and through some sacrifices. This book is not about a get-rich-quick-and-easy scheme. This book is about a get-much-better-off-over-time plan. Sacrifices bring positive reinforcement each week, every month, and especially when writing the last check to pay off the mortgage.

I believe any couple or individual in America is capable of paying off the mortgage in just a few years. Please remember, when you buy a house, the bank usually owns more of the house than you, for many years. This book shows you how to fulfill the American dream of owning your home—outright.

Kathy and I purchased our second home for $289,000 and paid off the mortgage in twenty-three months. That's right, less than two years. How? First, using our 100 percent equity from paying off the mortgage early on our first house to help get a relatively small mortgage ($50,000) for our second home. And second—the way to pay off both mortgages early—make large "extra to principal" (ETP) payments every month. But how were we able to make large ETP payments every month? More important, how will you be able to make large ETP payments every month?  Use the specific strategies and tactics Kathy and I used to truly own our home.  This is real life.

I approach owning a home as winning a war against the mortgage:  an all-out, coordinated effort to pay off the mortgage decades or many years ahead of schedule.  Mortgage victory!  The strategies relate to the overall plan:  the objectives, mortgage goal, and ultimate goal.  The tactics relate to winning individual battles, such as getting the smallest mortgage, the best mortgage rate, and the money for making big ETP payments by reducing expenses and reducing spending day-to-day, week-to-week, and month-to-month.  In addition, I emphasize the importance of maintaining an adequate amount of readily available money (liquid assets) for unexpected needs and planning for retirement.

The strategies and tactics necessary for mortgage victory are universal and benefit everybody.  Purchasing your first house?  In your home for a few or many years?  Perhaps it's tough just making the next mortgage (or rent) payment or saving enough money for a down payment.  Or, you can't work enough to get ends to meet: working and working to pay for your spending and spending.  Control and reduce expenses and spending and the ends become closer and easier to meet.  People have habits, personalities, and philosophies that help or hinder the war on the mortgage.  Variables, such as differences in state income and property taxes, and the prices of goods and services in various states, do not matter.  Carry out the strategies and tactics discussed in this book and you'll be much better off than if you (and people with similar circumstances) didn't use the plan.

The book reflects the gravity of the topic—war.  Recommendations are written like orders.  Total commitment is necessary for victory!

Fighting and winning the mortgage war is fun.  And, when you win all the battles, the ultimate victory is fabulous.  You forget about making monthly mortgage payments, take for granted you own your home outright and have no debt, and enjoy the benefits of your accomplishment.

# Chapter 1

# Who Benefits from This Book? Everyone

Everyone with a mortgage, everyone who wants a mortgage, and everyone in debt benefits from implementing the strategies and tactics described in this book. But, as they say (whoever "they" are), everything is relative.

## TINKs

In general, working couples with no children (two incomes and no kids—TINKs) benefit the most from this book. Next, working couples with one child. Then working couples with two children. In the mortgage war, no or fewer children allows you to put more money, more rapidly to paying off the mortgage (or saving for a down payment). It's important to emphasize, however, that even with children, the more mortgage battles won with extra to principal (ETP) payments, the better off the children in the long run.

Couples with one income and individuals with an income also benefit. Of course, one income achieves the advantages slower than two incomes.

Relatively speaking, TINKs (and others) with lower incomes benefit as much as TINKs with higher incomes. The TINKs with higher incomes usually have a greater mortgage in total dollars. The TINKs with lower incomes typically have a smaller mortgage in total dollars. The amount of the mortgage, however, is normally proportional to the income. Everyone pays off their mortgages at approximately the same faster rate.

## Which of the Following Applies to You?

Buying Your First Home

Before buying your first house, accumulate the largest down payment possible.  Not to buy a house more expensive than you can realistically afford, but to reduce the amount of money you have to borrow (the total principal) and the amount of the monthly mortgage payments (the principal plus interest). Borrow as little as possible and you have less principal to repay and less interest, because of the smaller principal.  Therefore, more money goes for ETP each month. Also, when you buy the house and begin to pay off the mortgage, you continue the same strategies and tactics used to accumulate the down payment.

A larger down payment appeals to the bank or mortgage company.  In addition to your credit history, and income history and future, the more you exceed the bank's minimum down payment requirement, the more favorably your application is received. Remember, you're not interested in making the bank's minimum percent (e.g., five percent) or minimum amount for the down payment; you're interested in the smallest mortgage.

Allowing more time to accumulate a larger down payment must be weighed against what's happening to the interest rates and prices of houses.  Interest rates going down?  Patiently amassing a greater down payment has an extra advantage, declining rates. However, lower interest rates usually result in an increased demand for houses, and prices may go up. Interest rates going up?  The increased amount of interest payments on the mortgage may eliminate any advantage in delaying the purchase in order to have a larger down payment.  But, if demand for houses decreases because of higher interest rates, prices may go down.  If interest rates are stable, having a larger down payment still has benefits.

The other major consideration in the amount of time allotted to saving for a large down payment:  finding a house that you love.  If you only like a house or rationalize about many problems with the house or property, you are much less likely to live happily ever after. Generally, you love either an existing house or condominium, or a house to be built.  Since you have no house to market, you can close relatively fast, assuming the seller can close soon and move out.  No house to market may be an advantage to the seller because the sale is not contingent on you selling your house. Construction of a house is seldom on schedule; usually you have extra time to build your down payment.

Selling One House and Buying Another Home (Sooner or Later)

If you (and a bank or mortgage company) own a house you are or will ever be selling when buying another home, calculate your equity in the your property.  The equity is simply the difference between the selling price  (not the "asking price") or value of your current house minus the amount of money you owe the bank in principal on your current house. You want your equity to be a large, positive number.

For example, if you're selling your present house for $150,000 and you owe the bank $85,000 in principal, then your equity in the house is $65,000 ($150,000 - $85,000). You use the equity, the $65,000, as the down payment, or part of the down payment, on the house you are purchasing. The more principal you have paid off, the more equity you have in your house before buying a new home.

Win this mortgage war, no longer owe any principal on your $150,000 house, and you have a $150,000 down payment on your new home.  The $150,000 allows you to purchase a wonderful new home—you can realistically afford—with a relatively small mortgage.  Enjoy your beautiful new home.

You Want to Eliminate All Debt

You love your home and plan to live happily ever after without moving. One problem: you hate the mortgage. Use the strategies and tactics; eliminate the mortgage and all other debt. You're debt-free!

You Need to Take Control of Financial Management Problems

Having trouble just making the basic mortgage payment each
month?  Are you always in debt?  Maybe you can't accumulate
anything for a down payment.  First, use the strategies and tactics
to control and improve your financial situation; then concentrate on
the mortgage war or saving for a down payment.

## Summary

Are you TINKs, waiting to start a family?  Would you like to own
your home outright and have no debt before having a child?
Want to pay off your mortgage many years ahead of schedule,
merely want a mortgage and home, or just want to get out of debt?
Whatever your situation you benefit from this book.  All you have
to do:  use the strategies and tactics.

# Chapter 2

# Philosophies, Principles, the Mindset, and Strategies for Mortgage Victory

As you read this book, ask yourself the crucial question: "Does this make sense?" When you believe the information and recommendations make sense, you are motivated and succeed.

Changes in your lifestyle and habits; necessary sacrifices to win the mortgage battles with large extra to principal (ETP) payments each month and the mortgage war. Are you willing and philosophically able to make the necessary lifestyle changes? You must believe the benefits of paying off the mortgage years or decades ahead of schedule are worth the sacrifices.

Here are some of my long-held philosophies and principles that helped me win the mortgage war—twice.

## Finite Resources

Unless you have a constant flow of unlimited income, you have finite resources. (If you enjoy unlimited income, you don't need this book. Stop reading and please get in touch with me.) You have a limited, relatively predictable take-home pay from wages or salary. You may also have bonuses, commissions, business profits, or tips, each of which may fluctuate, and interest or dividends. It doesn't matter if you take home $300 a week or $3,000 a week. Finite resources means a limit to the funds you have available when you choose to spend money or pay ETP.

## Priorities, Decisions, and Actions

The United States, a fabulous country where American citizens have many opportunities and choices. Life: one long series of many choices an decisions. But first you have to establish your priorities. You make decisions every day based on your priorities. The decisions you make lead to certain actions and behaviors, or not taking action. These actions, behaviors or lack of action have consequences—favorable or unfavorable—for which you are responsible. The most important factor is your priorities. Your priorities dictate your decisions, actions, and consequences.

With the right priorities, someone bringing home $300 a week has more money for ETP payments than a person with the wrong priorities bringing home $3,000 a week. Even if you take home $3,000 a week, if you decide to spend about as much as you make —even $3,000 a week—on jewelry, new suits and ties, dining out nightly, furniture, and television home shopping (every operator knows you personally), you have a large debt to pay with all the money you earn. You have no funds available to pay ETP. And if you constantly spend more money than you make, you have a deficit each month and a progressively increasing total debt.

The point: It's not how much money you make; it's how you use the money you make. How you use the money you make is based on your priorities; spend the money on unnecessary things or make ETP payments.

To win the mortgage war, having the most money available to pay ETP must be a top priority. The benefits of paying off the mortgage within a few years warrant being a top priority; the rewards justify the necessary sacrifices and lifestyle changes. Enthusiastically make the commitment to succeed.

## The Mindset

While your commitment to mortgage victory is essential over a few years, your money-saving mindset is critical on a daily basis. The American Heritage College Dictionary, 3rd ed. (Houghton Mifflin Co., 1993) definition of mindset is "1. A fixed mental attitude or disposition that predetermines a person's response to interpretations of situations. 2. An inclination or a habit." Establish a mindset to make the right money-saving decisions throughout every single day, and you have the money for large ETP payments.

## Strategies

The mortgage war is based on strategies and tactics. The tactics, which relate to the specific ways to accomplish the objectives described below, are discussed in detail in several chapters. Here, I focus on the strategies.

The strategies relate to the overall plan: the objectives, the mortgage goal and the ultimate goal.

## Objectives

The two major objectives: reduce expenses and reduce spending. I define expenses as necessary expenditures, such as heat, telephone, electricity, and supermarket food. I think of spending as discretionary expenditures; the products and services you purchase with the money you have available after expenses. Achieving both major objectives is within your control every day.

Another objective is to increase income. However, increasing income is probably not within your control on a day-to-day basis.

By significantly reducing expenses and spending, and periodically increasing income, you have as much money as possible for large ETP payments.

## Mortgage Goal

The mortgage goal: pay off your home mortgage, thereby win the mortgage war, as quickly as possible. Period. The larger the ETP payments, the faster you pay off your mortgage. When you win the mortgage war, you also reach the ultimate goal.

## Ultimate Goal

The ultimate goal: enjoy three enormous benefits of mortgage victory; the rewards for your sacrifices and lifestyle changes.

The first big benefit to enjoy is peace of mind.  You're debt-free; no more monthly payments of hundreds and hundreds of dollars. The house and land are yours and, when you pay your property (if applicable) and income taxes, nobody can take your home away from you. (You need to pay home owner's insurance, too.)  Lose your job, need to resign for personal reasons, an emergency strikes—don't worry about mortgage payments and the bank. Take for granted you own your home outright.  You have 100 percent equity.  If and when you want to move up in the world, you have the full value of the property to put toward your next house (minus sales commission, if any).  Glorious peace of mind.

The second big benefit is the use of your goal and priority philosophy and money-saving mindset.  They helped win the mortgage war; use them for new goals, priorities and decisions.  Now that you have no mortgage and no debt, what's your new goal?  Perhaps it's saving for your children's college tuition, buying a bigger and nicer home, or retiring early.  For Kathy and I, our goal—based on two profound personal experiences—spend more time together, especially on vacations. We achieve that goal every year.  But first things first. We established our mortgage goal, used our money-saving mindset over the years, and paid off two mortgages.  We continue to use our goal and priority philosophy and money-saving mindset and achieve our vacation goal—debt-free.  You will achieve your goal too.

The third big benefit is a great sense of pride in your long-term accomplishments. You sacrificed some pleasures and conveniences, and you were a smart shopper.  No one, no government programs, gave you anything.  No excuses, justifications or rationalizations (e.g., cheating on taxes because "everyone does it"). This is the test: Would you, your parents and children be happy and proud to read about all of your financial actions on the front page of the local newspaper and The New York Times?  You, your parents and children will be proud when you honestly earn and truly deserve everything you now enjoy.

## The Question

Does what I have said—the philosophies, principles and mindset, and the objectives, mortgage goal and ultimate goal—make sense to you? If so, you have taken the first, substantial step toward winning the mortgage war and achieving the ultimate goal.

The next step: read, understand and accept the tactics and strategies I discuss in this book. And then, the most worthwhile step, use the strategies and tactics on a day-to-day, month-to-month, and year-to-year basis. You will decrease your expenses and spending, take control of your finances, pay off your home mortgage many years or decades ahead of schedule, and enjoy the wonderful benefits of your accomplishments.

12  Win the Mortgage War

# Part II

# The Critical Numbers

# Chapter 3

# Mortgage Victory!
# My Example

Here's my real life example of winning the mortgage war twice, aggressively paying off the mortgages on my first and second houses. I paid off the mortgage on my first house in only six years. Then I used the 100 percent equity from my first house, $210,000, minus the sales commission, as part of the down payment for my second home. I added some reserve funds for the down payment of $239,000 and needed only a $50,000 mortgage when I purchased my second house for $289,000.

**The Details**

The mortgage for my second house was a fifteen-year, $50,000 mortgage at 9.95 percent interest. The basic monthly payment (basic principal plus interest) was $535.78. I paid the property taxes and the home owners insurance directly (not through the bank).

During the two years the mortgage was paid off, Kathy's and my combined gross income was about $79,500 a year. That's before federal income, social security, Medicare, state income and sales, and local property taxes.

Second Home Mortgage Victory

Table 3.1 documents the amount of the basic monthly payment of $535.78 that went to basic principal and interest, the amount of the ETP payments, and the principal balance.

## Table 3.1[a]
## Dave's Second Home Mortgage Victory

| Month | Basic Principal | Interest | Extra to Principal | Principal Balance |
|---|---|---|---|---|
| | | $82.92[b] | | $50,000.00 |
| 1 | $121.20 | 414.58 | $2,000 | 47,878.80 |
| 2 | 138.78 | 397.00 | 2,000 | 45,740.02 |
| 3 | 156.52 | 379.26 | 1,000 | 44,583.50 |
| 4 | 166.11 | 369.67 | 2,000 | 42,417.39 |
| 5 | 184.07 | 351.71 | 3,000 | 39,233.32 |
| 6 | 210.47 | 325.31 | 3,000 | 36,022.85 |
| 7 | 237.09 | 298.69 | 2,000 | 33,785.76 |
| 8 | 255.64 | 280.14 | 2,000 | 31,530.12 |
| 9 | 274.34 now > | 261.44 | 2,000 | 29,255.78 |
| 10 | 293.20 | 242.58 | 2,000 | 26,962.58 |
| 11 | 312.22 | 223.56 | 2,000 | 24,650.36 |
| 12 | 331.39 | 204.39 | 2,000 | 22,318.97 |
| 13 | 350.72 | 185.06 | 2,000 | 19,968.25 |
| 14 | 370.21 | 165.57 | 2,000 | 17,598.04 |
| 15 | 389.86 | 145.92 | 800 | 16,408.18 |
| 16 | 399.73 | 136.05 | 0 | 16,008.45 |
| 17 | 403.04 | 132.74 | 2,000 | 13,605.41 |
| 18 | 422.97 | 112.81 | 2,000 | 11,182.44 |
| 19 | 443.06 | 92.72 | 1,000 | 9,739.38 |
| 20 | 455.02 | 80.76 | 1,500 | 7,784.36 |
| 21 | 471.23 | 64.55 | 500 | 6,813.13 |
| 22 | 479.29 | 56.49 | 500 | 5,833.84 |
| 23 | $487.41 | $48.37 | $5,346.43 | PAID OFF! |

[a]The Table is a consolidated representation of payments, some ETP payments were made mid-month

[b]Prorated interest paid at closing for the first month

**Analysis:  The Wonderful News**

Please note that of the first basic payment of \$535.78, a colossal \$414.58 went to interest and only a meager \$121.20 went to principal.  That's \$293.38 more going to interest than principal.  However, with aggressive extra to principal (ETP) payments, the amount of the basic payment going to principal exceeded that paying interest after only a minuscule eight payments.  This accomplishment would have taken over eight years without ETP payments.

According to the bank's mortgage disclosure statement, I would have paid \$46,523.32 in finance charges alone over the full fifteen years of the mortgage: \$46,000 interest on a \$50,000 loan.  The interest actually paid over the two years: \$5,052.29.  I saved a fabulous \$41,471.03 or eighty-nine percent of the expected interest on the loan!

Also, I had 100 percent equity in my second home—and no more mortgage payments—after only two years.  Thirteen years earlier than if I just made the basic monthly mortgage payments.

Seeing the basic principal amounts go up, seeing the interest amounts go down, and most important, seeing the principal balance plummet, provided positive reinforcement each month that all my efforts and sacrifices were well worthwhile.  The strategies and tactics worked.  I won the mortgage battle every month with large ETP payments, and I won the mortgage war for my second house in only two years!

**You Can Too**

You can win the mortgage war on your first or current house in a few to several years.  You do not—repeat do not—have to make \$2,000 ETP payments a month to achieve victory.  It's all relative; your ETP payments may be more or less than mine.  Your objective:  Make the largest ETP payments possible for you, using the money saved by prioritizing, sacrificing, and reducing expenses and spending.  If you are TINKs (two incomes and no kids), try to live on one income, as I did, and put the larger income toward the mortgage war.

After your first mortgage victory, if you want to move to a nicer home, use the 100 percent equity to buy your second home with a relatively small mortgage. Then use the same strategies and tactics to pay off the mortgage on the second house in two years. I've done it. You can too.

# Chapter 4

# Finances 101: Paying Off Your Mortgage Makes Financial Sense

This is a two-part course: Part One covers the strictly financial advantages of paying off your mortgage extremely early and Part Two covers the importance of having funds available for unanticipated needs (liquid assets) and planning for retirement.

**Part One**

Some people may say it doesn't make financial sense to pay off the mortgage early. They usually have two arguments: The loss of the federal tax deduction for mortgage interest payments and making better use of your money by investing than paying extra to principal (ETP). I play both devil's advocate and me.

The Loss of the Federal Income Tax Deduction

The devil's advocate says, "I have less of a federal income tax deduction as I pay less mortgage interest and I lose my federal tax deduction when the mortgage is paid off."

I say, "That's true, but—and it's a big but." My argument, based purely on finances: you are better off without federal tax deductions from mortgage interest payments. Here's why. First, think of your federal tax rate (or bracket) based on income, such as fifteen percent, thirty-one percent, or thirty-six percent, with increasing income.

Then calculate the net effect of paying mortgage interest and taking the federal income tax deduction. You pay one dollar to the bank in mortgage interest to get a one dollar tax deduction (not tax credit) on your federal taxes. If you're in the thirty-six percent federal tax bracket, for every dollar in interest paid you save thirty-six cents on your federal taxes. That's right. You pay one dollar in interest to save thirty-six cents in federal tax. Therefore, to enjoy the wonderful federal tax deduction, it costs you—repeat costs you —a net sixty-four cents. A lower income costs you more. If you're in the fifteen percent tax bracket, it costs you a net eighty-five cents for every dollar of mortgage interest you pay. Now multiply that by the tens of thousands of dollars in interest you pay over the life of the loan.

My proposal

You give me (or the bank in interest payments) ten thousand dollars and I (or the federal government in tax deductions) give you thirty-six hundred dollars or fifteen hundred dollars. How long do you want to do that? If that arrangement doesn't sound good, pay off your mortgage as soon as possible, eliminate paying interest, and keep the ten thousand dollars and more.

Make Better Use of Your Money by Investing than
Paying Extra to Principal

The devil's advocate says, "I can invest the money I would pay extra to principal and earn more interest and dividends than the ETP would save in mortgage interest, especially with low interest rates and the tax deduction combined."

I say, "Perhaps, but I prefer a sure thing to a gamble." For every dollar you pay ETP you eliminate a dollar of principal debt and reduce all future interest payments; therefore, all basic payments have a larger amount going to principal. When you pay off the mortgage you entirely eliminate the debt; gone forever. That's guaranteed. Even if you lose your job, you do not lose your house. You also have 100 percent equity in your house. That's guaranteed. You no longer have any mortgage interest to pay. That's guaranteed.

If you invest your ETP money, what are the guarantees? Your net earnings in interest and dividends from investments minus any federal and state income taxes on the profits, plus the federal mortgage interest tax deduction, must exceed the mortgage interest rate and, more importantly, the actual mortgage interest dollars paid over the life of the loan (which is as long as you own the house, or fifteen years or thirty years).

What are the alternative investment options? The bank savings accounts and money market funds are essentially guaranteed, but pay low interest at this time. Bonds, notes, and treasury bills have a guaranteed return if held to maturity, but fluctuate in value until then. Historically, the stock market provides the best long-term return on investment. Picking individual stocks can be tricky. Mutual funds may be less chancy, depending on the particular fund's investment strategy. But increased potential growth means increased risk for loss.

To determine the net return on investment, you must deduct the federal and state income taxes (if applicable) from any gains. Then you can factor in the federal tax deduction from paying mortgage interest. Now subtract the effect of inflation over the years on your net gains. Of course if, even with good intentions, you end up spending the ETP funds meant for alternative investments, you don't have to worry about inflation adversely affecting your net gains.

When the devil's advocate considers investing money that should go to ETP payments, I emphasize three crucial points: the colossal amount of interest dollars you pay during the early to middle (plus) years of the loan period, the minuscule amount of equity in your home realized with basic mortgage payments versus increased equity with aggressive ETP payments, and the unlimited investment options when the mortgage war is won.

It is critical to remember: You pay a gigantic number of dollars in interest early in the mortgage period. The overwhelming majority of your basic monthly mortgage payment goes to interest for many years. Theoretically, the lower the mortgage interest rate the better the chance that the net return on ETP dollars used for investments will exceed the mortgage interest percentage, over the life of a loan—if you do not sell your house before the end of the fifteen-year or thirty-year loan period.  If you move in seven years (the average length of home ownership), you pay much more than fifty percent in interest with every month's basic mortgage payment, no matter what the mortgage interest rate.  You must have a phenomenal return on investment to match the dollars in interest you pay if you do not aggressively pay ETP early in the loan period. Do you know how many years it is before the amount to principal exceeds the amount to interest for your basic monthly payment in your mortgage?  About twenty-two years for a thirty-year loan.

Make only basic payments and you reduce the amount of principal owed and, therefore, increase the equity in your house, at a lame snail's pace. With aggressive ETP payments, the equity in your home increases dramatically. The greater home equity represents a big, splendid part of your net assets (all you own minus all you owe). If mortgage interest rates fall, your increased equity helps get approval for refinancing, even if housing values fall. If you refinance or get a low rate from the start, put even more money to ETP payments, not to alternative investments.

When you win the mortgage war, you have the money you paid every month in basic mortgage payments plus the ETP money to use for your ultimate goal, and for investing and saving. With your spend-less-money mindset, you are used to living without the mortgage money and can use the money saved to rapidly increase your investments. That adds up fast.  And you have 100 percent equity in your house too!  Other than a relatively small mortgage on your next house (if desired), you should not have to borrow money again.

Crucial Financial Objective

Get the maximum benefit from ETP payments:   make ETP payments as early in the life of the loan as possible (start the first month of the loan or today) and make ETP payments as large as possible.

The portion of each month's basic payment that pays off principal and that goes to interest depends on the outstanding principal and, therefore, all the previous payments to reduce the outstanding principal.  This fact works in your favor when you start ETP payments on day one or early in the loan and when large ETP payments reduce the outstanding principal rapidly. You'll be amazed at the results of large ETP payments, especially early in the life of the loan.

It's true that even small ETP payments reduce the life of a mortgage by a few years and save interest dollars; however, I don't want to minimize the mortgage goal, reduce the size of ETP payments, and drag out the mortgage. Win monthly mortgage battles by striving for high standards and large ETP payments, not by settling for low standards and small ETP payments. Mortgage victory cuts many years, possibly more than twenty years, off the term of the loan and, more importantly, saves tens of thousands of dollars, possibly over $100,000, in interest.

**Part Two**

While I focus on the many benefits of winning the mortgage war, it's important to emphasize two additional priorities: having money available for unanticipated needs (liquid assets) and planning for retirement.

Liquid Assets

Prepare for a rainy day; have sufficient liquid assets. By liquid assets I mean funds in a savings account or money market account that you contribute to periodically and can use on short notice.

A savings account or money market account may not pay a lot of interest, but the money is readily available for an unanticipated need and liquid assets are not meant as investments. Liquid assets don't include: certificates of deposit (CDs), which have maturity dates and are not readily available without penalties; stocks or mutual funds, which may be low when you need the money; and bonds, which may be low when you need the money and have maturity dates.

The amount of liquid assets you need to maintain depends on your income. How much money you can set aside? Five thousand to ten thousand dollars is usually sufficient, especially with the rapidly increasing equity in your home available for a big emergency.

Liquid assets are intended for unanticipated needs, not for buying a living room set or television. For those and other more expensive needs, set up an account and save gradually—but not in place of ETP payments (see Chapter Four).

Sufficient liquid assets are important. They give you peace of mind, let you preserve your long-term investments, and let you focus on winning the mortgage war.

Planning for Retirement

Assure a happy, comfortable retirement by planning for retirement early. In fact, plan early for retirement and be financially able to retire early, especially if that's your ultimate goal.

Please note: Tax laws are subject to change. Obtain current Internal Revenue Service (IRS) publications or information on the following retirement plans.

First step

First, sign up for your employer-sponsored retirement plan, such as a 401(k) plan, if offered; establish a Keogh (HR 10) plan, if you are self-employed; or open an Individual Retirement Arrangement (IRA) account.

401(k) Plan. The 401(k) plan has many advantages. Your contributions to a 401(k) plan are tax-deferred, not taxed until retirement at age sixty-five. If withdrawn earlier there's a penalty. Your contributions are taken from your gross income (e.g., from your weekly pay or salary) and diverted to the 401(k) plan before the gross income is reported to the IRS; thereby reducing your taxable income. And you don't see or miss the money. The amount of the contributions is usually a percentage of your income; so as your income increases your contributions increase. Also, your contributions are often matched, dollar for dollar or cents on the dollar, by your employer. You choose how these combined funds are invested from a selection of investment options. Contribute the maximum possible that is matched by your employer. The 401(k) plan: an easy, painless, and effective way to save for retirement.

Keogh Plan. If you are self-employed start a Keogh (HR 10) plan for retirement. On your federal income tax form, you can deduct your contributions to the plan, within certain limits.

Individual Retirement Arrangement (IRA) Account. If you (and your spouse, if applicable) were not covered by any retirement plan, either employer or self-employed, you may be able to establish an IRA account and deduct your contributions on your federal income tax form. If you qualify for a deduction, contribute the maximum amount you can use as a deduction. If you do or do not qualify for a deduction, you can still contribute to an IRA and the money you earn from the IRA contributions is not taxed until you receive the funds, at age sixty-five or earlier with a penalty.

Kathy and I used to contribute $2,000 each to our individual IRAs before the tax laws changed and we couldn't deduct the $4,000 on our federal income tax form. Because the IRA funds are tied up until we are sixty-five years old, we now invest in a bond fund that's free of state and federal income taxes. This is not an IRA; so this money is available for early retirement. Then we will be taxed on the reinvested dividends, not on the original investments, which were made with after-tax income.

Investment options

Whether you participate in a specific retirement plan or save for retirement on your own, you must select the how the money you set aside for retirement is invested. Financial experts usually say: The younger you are the more aggressive the investment strategy and the older you are the more conservative the investment strategy. Generally, that's a good strategy.

When younger, you can afford to take risks with the hope of bigger returns on investments over the long-term. Investments with a growth goal have ups and downs along the way, but usually yield the highest return over the long-term. Be patient and don't look at the financial pages for the next couple of decades.

When older, and closer to retirement, you want to make sure the retirement money is available in a few years, even with smaller returns on your investments. You want to ensure income, not risk your life's savings. Investments with an income goal are best when close to retirement.

I emphasize another investment strategy, perhaps the most important: The sleep test. Invest in a way you are most comfortable and you can sleep through the night. Whatever your age, do your investment homework, get several opinions, know the risks and benefits, and make a decision that allows you to sleep well every night. Which of the following would be worse? You invest in a growth mutual fund and lose a lot of money while the income fund steadily increases, or you invest in an income mutual fund whose value creeps up while the growth fund skyrockets up? You should have a somewhat diversified portfolio anyway, which could include balanced funds.

With retirement funds always think tax-deferred, tax-deferred, tax-deferred. Even though tax-deferred investments usually have a lower return than taxable investments; it's the net return that counts. But remember, there's no need for a tax-deferred fund for an IRA account, 401(k) plan, or Keogh plan; they're already tax-deferred.

No home mortgage

Paying off your mortgage years or decades early and being debt-free helps a lot for those planning an early retirement. With no mortgage, most or all of your discretionary funds goes to a retirement account(s). Relatively soon you have one hundred percent equity in your home, no debt, and a large retirement reserve: the perfect combination for early, comfortable retirement.

You have completed the course. It's now time to take the final exam.

**Final Exam for Finances 101**

Multiple choice.  Choose the one best answer.

Which of the following statements is true?

a.  Depending on your tax bracket, you pay—it costs you—a dollar in mortgage interest to save a mere fifteen cents to thirty-six cents in federal tax.

b.   Beginning the first month, the vast majority of your basic monthly mortgage payments is strictly paying interest—for many years.  Therefore, it's crucial to make ETP payments as early as possible in the life of the mortgage and as large as possible.

c.  You should have sufficient liquid assets for unanticipated needs.

d.  Planning and investing for your retirement early and wisely is important to assure an early and comfortable retirement.

e.  All of the above are true.

If you picked "e." congratulations you passed the course with a 100 on the final exam.  You are invited to take Finances 102 in the next chapter. Finances 102 documents several specific, excellent outcomes of  making (and not making) various ETP payments.

28   Win the Mortgage War

# Finances 102: Slash Many Years and Tens of Thousands of Dollars Off Your Mortgage

The Mortgage War. This chapter documents why I call aggressively paying off your mortgage with large extra to principal (ETP) payments as early in the term of the loan as possible, the mortgage war.

As discussed in Finances 101, starting with the first payment and continuing for many years, here's what happens to your basic monthly payment: you pay a massive amount to interest (the lender's profits) and a minuscule amount to pay off the principal, the loan.

### The Proof: Tables and Figures

The following tables and figures allow you to see the specific financial consequences of not battling the mortgage—just going along with the standard, basic monthly payments of interest and principal—you endure staggering debt for many years and take a severe financial beating. Look what you're doing to yourself.

You also see the fabulous financial benefits of fighting and winning the mortgage war: slashing many years and tens of thousands of dollars off your mortgage. Look what you can do for yourself with ETP payments.

Total Interest Cost

Table 5.1 presents the staggering amount paid to interest alone over the term of fifteen-year and thirty-year mortgages at various interest rates and loan amounts.

As you approach ten percent interest and above, over the life of every thirty-year loan (regardless of the amount borrowed), you pay in interest twice as much as you borrowed. For a fifteen-year loan, you pay in interest as much as you borrowed.

The amount of interest paid is terrible, but it's worse that the overwhelming majority of the interest is paid in the earlier part of the loan. An example is shown in Table 5.2.

Normal Payment Schedule for a Thirty-Year Loan

Table 5.2 shows what happens with a typical thirty-year, $50,000 mortgage at 7.5% interest—without ETP payments.

As you see, the total payment each month is $349.61. Of the first $349.61 payment, $312.50 pays interest and only $37.11 goes to pay off the principal owed. The amount of the monthly payment paying interest is greater than the amount paying off the principal for more than 240 payments or twenty years.

If you do not make ETP payments: After one year, you will have paid $3,734.37 in interest, and still owe $49,539.05 in principal. After sixty payments, five years, you will have paid over $18,000 in interest, and still owe over $47,000 on a $50,000 loan. After 120 payments, ten years, you will have paid over $35,000 in interest, and still owe over $43,000. So, if you move in ten years, you paid five times more interest than principal and you still must pay off the $43,000 in remaining principal on this house before you can get a loan for your next house.

After 240 payments, twenty years, you will have paid the bank over $63,000 in interest and still owe the lender over $29,000 in principal . . . on a $50,000 loan. And, if you stay in the house for the full thirty years, plodding along with the basic monthly payments—no ETP payments—you will have paid over $75,000 in interest, just interest.

Table 5.1
**Total Interest Cost**

| Loan amount | 6.0% rate | | 7.0% rate | | 8.0% rate | | 9.0% rate | | 10.0% rate | | 11.0% rate | |
|---|---|---|---|---|---|---|---|---|---|---|---|---|
| | 15 yr | 30 yr | 15 yr | 30 yr | 15 yr | 30 yr | 15 yr | 30 yr | 15 yr | 30 yr | 15 yr | 30 yr |
| $20,000 | $10,379 | $23,168 | $12,358 | $27,902 | $14,403 | $32,831 | $16,514 | $37,933 | $18,686 | $43,185 | $20,917 | $48,567 |
| 25,000 | 12,974 | 28,960 | 15,447 | 34,877 | 18,004 | 41,039 | 20,642 | 47,416 | 23,357 | 53,981 | 26,147 | 60,709 |
| 30,000 | 15,568 | 34,751 | 18,537 | 41,853 | 21,605 | 49,247 | 24,770 | 56,899 | 28,029 | 64,778 | 31,376 | 72,851 |
| 35,000 | 18,163 | 40,543 | 21,626 | 48,828 | 25,206 | 57,454 | 28,899 | 66,382 | 32,700 | 75,574 | 36,606 | 84,993 |
| 40,000 | 20,758 | 46,335 | 24,716 | 55,804 | 28,807 | 65,662 | 33,027 | 75,866 | 37,372 | 86,370 | 41,835 | 97,135 |
| 45,000 | 23,352 | 52,127 | 27,805 | 62,779 | 32,408 | 73,870 | 37,156 | 85,349 | 42,043 | 97,167 | 47,064 | 109,276 |
| 50,000 | 25,947 | 57,919 | 30,895 | 69,754 | 36,009 | 82,078 | 41,284 | 94,832 | 46,714 | 107,963 | 52,294 | 121,418 |
| 55,000 | 28,542 | 63,711 | 33,984 | 76,730 | 39,610 | 90,285 | 45,412 | 104,315 | 51,386 | 118,759 | 57,523 | 133,560 |
| 60,000 | 31,137 | 69,503 | 37,073 | 83,705 | 43,210 | 98,493 | 49,541 | 113,798 | 56,057 | 129,555 | 62,752 | 145,702 |
| 65,000 | 33,731 | 75,295 | 40,163 | 90,681 | 46,811 | 106,701 | 53,669 | 123,282 | 60,729 | 140,352 | 67,982 | 157,844 |
| 70,000 | 36,326 | 81,087 | 43,252 | 97,656 | 50,412 | 114,909 | 57,798 | 132,765 | 65,400 | 151,148 | 73,211 | 169,985 |
| 75,000 | 38,921 | 86,879 | 46,342 | 104,632 | 54,013 | 123,116 | 61,926 | 142,248 | 70,072 | 161,944 | 78,441 | 182,127 |
| 80,000 | 41,515 | 92,671 | 49,431 | 111,607 | 57,614 | 131,324 | 66,054 | 151,731 | 74,743 | 172,741 | 83,670 | 194,269 |
| 85,000 | 44,110 | 98,462 | 52,521 | 118,583 | 61,215 | 139,532 | 70,183 | 161,215 | 79,415 | 183,537 | 88,899 | 206,411 |
| 90,000 | 46,705 | 104,254 | 55,610 | 125,558 | 64,816 | 147,740 | 74,311 | 170,698 | 84,086 | 194,333 | 94,129 | 218,553 |
| 95,000 | 49,300 | 110,046 | 58,700 | 132,533 | 68,417 | 155,947 | 78,440 | 180,181 | 88,757 | 205,129 | 99,358 | 230,695 |
| 100,000 | 51,894 | 115,838 | 61,789 | 139,509 | 72,017 | 164,155 | 82,568 | 189,664 | 93,429 | 215,926 | 104,587 | 242,836 |
| 105,000 | 54,489 | 121,630 | 64,879 | 146,484 | 75,618 | 172,363 | 86,696 | 199,147 | 98,100 | 226,722 | 109,817 | 254,978 |
| 110,000 | 57,084 | 127,422 | 67,968 | 153,460 | 79,219 | 180,571 | 90,825 | 208,631 | 102,772 | 237,518 | 115,046 | 267,120 |
| 115,000 | 59,678 | 133,214 | 71,057 | 160,435 | 82,820 | 188,779 | 94,953 | 218,114 | 107,443 | 248,315 | 120,276 | 279,262 |
| 120,000 | 62,273 | 139,006 | 74,147 | 167,411 | 86,421 | 196,986 | 99,082 | 227,597 | 112,115 | 259,111 | 125,505 | 291,404 |
| 125,000 | 64,868 | 144,798 | 77,236 | 174,386 | 90,022 | 205,194 | 103,210 | 237,080 | 116,786 | 269,907 | 130,734 | 303,546 |
| 130,000 | 67,462 | 150,590 | 80,326 | 181,362 | 93,623 | 213,402 | 107,338 | 246,563 | 121,458 | 280,703 | 135,964 | 315,687 |
| 135,000 | 70,057 | 156,382 | 83,415 | 188,337 | 97,223 | 221,610 | 111,467 | 256,047 | 126,129 | 291,500 | 141,193 | 327,829 |
| 140,000 | 72,652 | 162,173 | 86,505 | 195,312 | 100,824 | 229,817 | 115,595 | 265,530 | 130,800 | 302,296 | 146,422 | 339,971 |
| 145,000 | 75,247 | 167,965 | 89,594 | 202,288 | 104,425 | 238,025 | 119,724 | 275,013 | 135,472 | 313,092 | 151,652 | 352,113 |
| 150,000 | 77,841 | 173,757 | 92,684 | 209,263 | 108,026 | 246,233 | 123,852 | 284,496 | 140,143 | 323,889 | 156,881 | 364,255 |

Table 5.2

**Normal Payment Schedule for a Thirty-Year Loan**

$50,000 loan, 30-year term, interest rate = 7.5%

| Payment Number | Total Payment | Interest Payment | Principal Payment | Interest Paid to Date | Remaining Principal Owed |
|---|---|---|---|---|---|
| | | | | *loan amount:* | $50,000.00 |
| 1 | $349.61 | $312.50 | $37.11 | $312.50 | $49,962.89 |
| 2 | 349.61 | 312.27 | 37.34 | 624.77 | 49,925.55 |
| 3 | 349.61 | 312.03 | 37.58 | 936.80 | 49,887.97 |
| 4 | 349.61 | 311.80 | 37.81 | 1,248.60 | 49,850.16 |
| 5 | 349.61 | 311.56 | 38.05 | 1,560.16 | 49,812.11 |
| 12 (1 yr) | 349.61 | 309.87 | 39.74 | 3,734.37 | 49,539.05 |
| 60 (5 yrs) | 349.61 | 296.01 | 53.60 | 18,285.13 | 47,308.53 |
| 120 (10 yrs) | 349.61 | 271.72 | 77.89 | 35,350.22 | 43,397.02 |
| 180 (15 yrs) | 349.61 | 236.41 | 113.20 | 50,642.24 | 37,712.44 |
| 240 (20 yrs) | 349.61 | 185.10 | 164.51 | 63,357.42 | 29,451.02 |
| 300 (25 yrs) | 349.61 | 110.52 | 239.09 | 72,327.84 | 17,444.84 |
| 360 (30 yrs) | 345.91 | 2.15 | 343.76 | 75,855.90 | 0.00 |

The canyon difference between amounts going to interest and to principal, especially for the first twenty years of the loan term, is illustrated in Figure 5.1.

The Two Parts of the Mortgage Payment Through the Life of the Loan

Figure 5.1 graphically shows the thirty-year, $50,000 mortgage at 7.5% interest described in Table 2. The basic monthly payment: look how much goes to interest, how little goes to pay off the principal, and for how many years.

Principal Still Owed Through the Life of the Loan

Figure 5.2 lets you see how much principal is still owed on a thirty-year, $100,000 mortgage, for various interest rates, with only basic monthly payments, and no ETP payments.

Look at the bottom of the figure, labeled "Year." Find the number of years you have made regular payments, follow the vertical line up to find your interest rate, then read across to the left to see how much more principal you still owe (a ruler may help at times).

For example, say you have an eight percent interest mortgage and have been making basic payments (no ETP) for ten years. Find 10 on the bottom, Year line and follow the line up to the 8% curve. Now (you may want to sit down), read across to the left and see that you still owe about $85,000. After ten years of payments you paid off about $15,000 on a $100,000 loan. Confirm this with your monthly statement, looking at the "principal balance" or call your lender.

Here's the big point: Look how much principal you will owe for many, many years to come. After ten more years of faithful basic payments, you will still owe $60,000 on the $100,000 mortgage. How long will it take to pay off half of the principal? Look at the "Principal Owed" column and find $50,000, read across the horizontal line, find the 8% curve, and read down: about twenty-three and a half years, approximately 282 payments, just to pay off half of the principal.

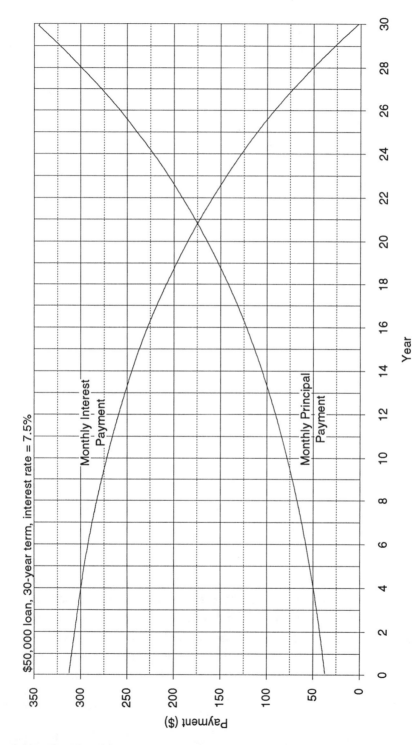

Figure 5.1  **The Two Parts of the Mortgage Payment Through the Life of the Loan**

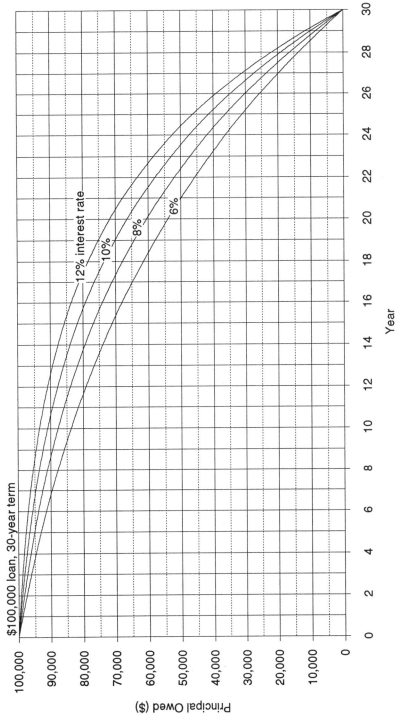

Figure 5.2 **Principal Still Owed Through the Life of the Loan**

If you sell the house early in the term of the loan, you have essentially paid only interest monthly for as many years and you still must repay almost all the principal.

Tables 5.1 and 5.2 and Figures 5.1 and 5.2 are the reasons you need to wage the mortgage war. Use all the strategies and tactics—every day—and win the monthly mortgage battles: make the largest ETP payments as early in the term of the loan as possible. The benefits of winning the mortgage battles every month—in interest saved and years saved—are clearly illustrated in the following figures.

Total Interest Saved Based on Extra to Principal Payments (Thirty-Year Loan and Fifteen-Year Loan)

Figures 5.3A and 5.3B show you how much interest you save on a $50,000 loan, at various interest rates; making various ETP payments, starting with the first payment and making the same ETP payment each month.

For instance, you have an eight percent interest, thirty-year mortgage and make $400 a month ETP payments. On Figure 5.3A (Thirty-Year Loan), find the "400" on the bottom "Extra to Principal Payment Per Month ($)" line, read up to the 8% curve, and read across to the left to the "Total Interest Saved ($)" line. With $400 ETP payments every month, you save approximately $60,000 in interest over the life of the loan, which is significantly shortened. With $800 a month ETP payments, you save almost $75,000 over the life of the loan, again significantly shortened.

For loan amounts other than $50,000, Figures 5.3A and B are still useful, except the ETP payments and total interest saved are adjusted proportionate to the loan amount.  For example, for a $100,000 loan (twice as much), doubling any ETP payment shown would result in twice the total interest savings shown.

Years Paying Mortgage Based on Extra to Principal Payments (Thirty-Year Loan and Fifteen-Year Loan)

To see how many, that is how few, years of pay the mortgage with ETP payments see Figures 5.4A and 5.4B. For the examples above, on Figure 5.4A (Thirty-Year Loan), find the "400" on the bottom "Extra to Principal Payment Per Month ($)" line, read up to the curve (one curve fits all interest rates from six percent to twelve percent for a $50,000 loan), and read across to the left to the "Years Paying Mortgage" line. With $400 ETP payments every month, you pay off the thirty-year mortgage in seven, that's right, seven years. No mortgage in seven years! With $800 a month ETP payments, you pay off the mortgage in four years. No mortgage, your house outright, 100 percent equity. Four years.

Your Loan

To use Figures 5.4A and 5.4B for your loan use the following equation:

$$ETP_{Your} = \frac{(Your\ Loan\ Amount) \times ETP_1}{50,000}$$

where:

ETP$_1$ is the ETP value shown in either Figure 5.4A or 5.4B, and

ETP$_{Your}$ is your actual ETP payment that reduces the term to the same amount shown in Figure 5.4A or 5.4B

For example, Figure 5.4B shows an ETP payment of $400 reduces the term of a thirty-year, $50,000 loan to seven years. If your loan amount is actually $75,000, then the ETP payment that reduces your loan to seven years is:

$$ETP_{Your} = \frac{(Actual\ Loan\ Amount) \times ETP1}{50,000}$$

$$= \frac{(\$75,000) \times 400}{50,000}$$

$$= \$600$$

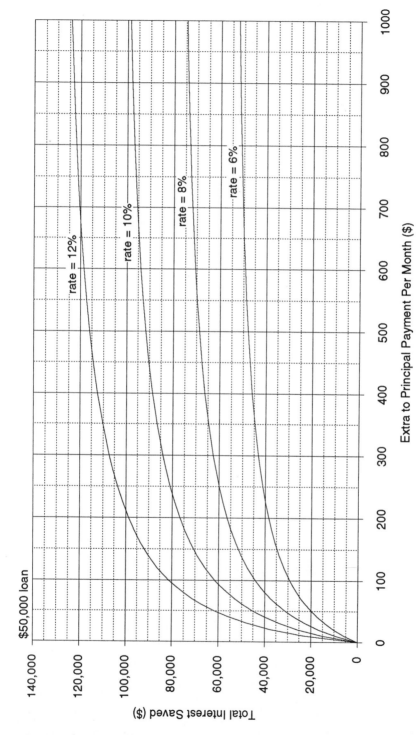

Figure 5.3A  Total Interest Saved Based on Extra to Principal Payments (Thirty-Year Loan)

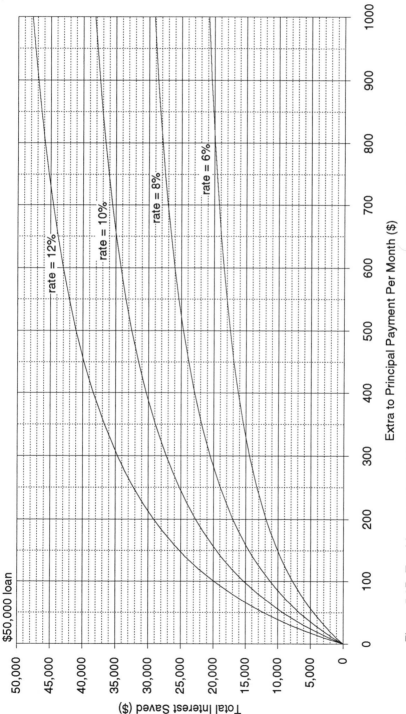

Figure 5.3B  Total Interest Saved Based on Extra to Principal Payments (Fifteen-Year Loan)

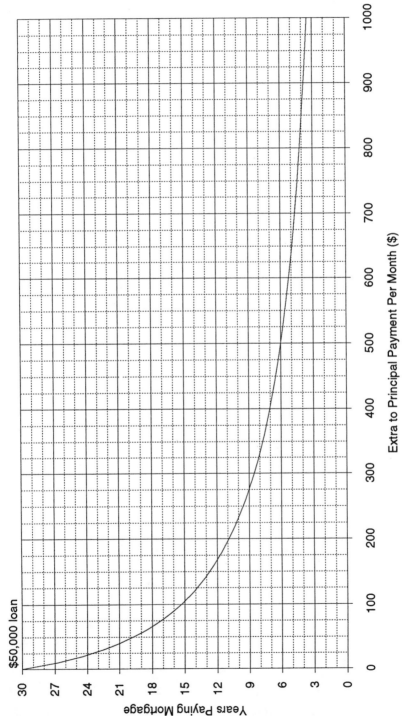

Figure 5.4A  Years Paying Mortgage Based on Extra to Principal Payments (Thirty-Year Loan)

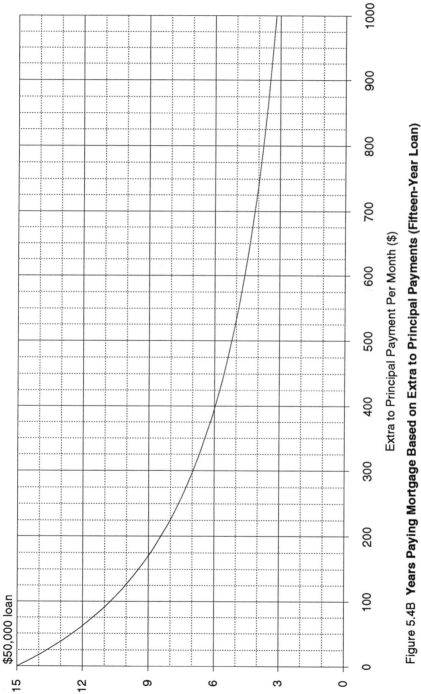

Figure 5.4B  Years Paying Mortgage Based on Extra to Principal Payments (Fifteen-Year Loan)

Just six hundred dollars a month in ETP payments cuts twenty-three years—twenty-three years—off a thirty-year loan. The tables and figures clearly demonstrate why lenders make profits at your expense, your interest dollars. Did your bank inform you that you could save $60,000 or $75,000 dollars in interest and twenty-three years or twenty-six years on a thirty-year, $50,000 loan? No? Well, now you know.

Examine the tables and figures and you will know why the mortgage war is necessary for your financial well-being.

## Summary

The tables and figures speak for themselves. If you just make basic monthly payments, the lender gets tens of thousands of your interest dollars and the lender wins the mortgage war. When you make monthly ETP payments as large and as early as possible, you win the mortgage battles every month and you win the mortgage war.

When you win the mortgage war in four or six years, you stop paying interest dollars, own the house outright, and use the wonderful 100 percent equity to buy a new house with a small mortgage. A mortgage you can, as I did, pay off in two years.

You will have the money necessary to make large ETP payments by using the winning tactics to reduce expenses and reduce spending. These tactics are described in the following section.

# Part III

# The Winning Tactics

## Reduce Expenses and Spending

# Chapter 6

# The Nine Commandments of Purchasing

There is a fundamental mindset for any and all purchases, from buying a candy bar to buying a car: The less money you spend, the more money you have to pay off the mortgage. Winning the mortgage war is the priority. Maintain the spend-less-money mindset, for small, medium, and large purchases, and saving money is second nature, easy, and its own positive reinforcement.

The objectives of the spend-less-money mindset are to reduce and minimize spending (mostly) and expenses (some apply) every day. Expenses relates to basic necessities, such as supermarket food, telephone, electricity, and gas or oil. Spending relates to your discretionary funds; the money you have a choice how to spend after expenses.

If you rationalize and make exceptions to the spend-less-money mindset, you lose individual spending battles and delay the mortgage victory or lose the war. (The only legitimate exception is medical necessity, of course.) Once you start to rationalize, you risk of making more and more exceptions. Therefore, make any exceptions only after careful thought, considering the alternatives and consequences, and never on impulse.

Spending less of your hard-earned money involves several fundamental tactics. I modestly call these tactics the Nine Commandments of Purchasing.

## The Nine Commandments of Purchasing

Know the Difference between Need and Want

If You Can Not Afford It, Do Not Buy It

Do Your Homework

Avoid Purchasing Cheap Products and Services—Cheap Can Be Expensive

Minimize Buying Convenience Goods and Services—Convenience Is Usually Costly

Always Think Value, Value, Value

Patience Please—Buy Everything on a Good or Great Sale or Discount

Use VISA or MasterCard Whenever Possible (Really)

Keep Accurate Records

## Know the Difference between Need and Want

When you're thinking about buying (or doing) something, ask yourself, "Do I really need this?"  The more expensive the item (or activity), the more important the question. I'm not saying only buy things related to food, clothing and shelter. Your definition of "need" has to be reasonable. The objective is to accept sacrifices, not endure hardships.

For me/us, in addition to the basics, I need a nice stereo, a big color television, a VCR, two automobiles, a computer, and time together on vacation.  I may want, but I do not need, the most expensive stereo system or the biggest TV in the country.

Base your determination of need to purchase anything, particularly something expensive, on your mortgage goal and priorities.

Be objective and don't rationalize. Do you just "want" the item or do you really "need" the item? Surprise! You can live happily without certain things, especially when you focus on the mortgage and ultimate goals. Self-control and self-discipline feel good and pay off.

I/we really do not need to spend money on many things. At the risk of offending some nice businesses and industries, things I/we don't do include: dine out or take-out meals (only on rare occasions [other than when away on vacation]), buy gifts for each other for any reason, buy fresh flowers (even for special occasions), buy jewelry (only rarely and inexpensive—support crafts), have Kathy's hair regularly "done," or have my shirts commercially laundered. Dollars add up fast when spent routinely over a long period of time. We've saved many thousands of dollars by knowing these and other things are really only wanted and not needed.

Think about your own habits and practices. You may not realize how much these habits you take for granted actually cost. Make a list of the things you do routinely, periodically, or occasionally in a typical week and month. How much do you spend on these habits each month and in a year? How many of those activities do you truly need? Again, base your determination of need on your mortgage goal and priorities. How much could you decrease spending (and use to pay off the mortgage) each month and year by eliminating activities you could live without?

Please be objective and don't rationalize. For example, do you absolutely need to go to the movies every week or every other week? And do you "get a bite to eat" before the show? Plus pay for parking at a city theater? Add it all up, then multiply by the number of times you go to the movies in a year. This amount of money is the annual spending on just one activity, among many. If you eliminate the total spending on movies (and other nonessential activities), you would put that money to the mortgage war. I'm sure you would use the additional time for enjoyable, free (or much, much less expensive) alternative activities. You don't have to live like a monk to reduce spending.

Focus strictly on your priorities when reviewing your list of habits. If you find yourself saying, "That would be nice" or "I want to do this," you know those activities are really not needed. Estimate the total annual drain on your funds for these nonessential habits and practices.

Resist the temptation to rationalize and say, "It's only thirty dollars a week," for one activity. Thirty dollars each week is about fifteen hundred dollars a year, just for one activity.  It all adds up and up and up.

Naturally, some of the alternative plans have costs. If you dine at home instead of a restaurant, the food still costs money. But you save on the tip and avoid paying for the restaurant's wonderful atmosphere, superb chef, business overhead, and profit. Not to mention the meal taxes and parking, if applicable.

Also, resist the temptation to rationalize that you work hard and you deserve to spend your money on nice things, little luxuries, personal rewards, and anything you want. I agree you work hard; you deserve to have your hard-earned money go to win the mortgage war and achieve the ultimate goal.  First things first: eliminate debt. Then your income—100 percent of your income (after expenses)—goes to your ultimate goal, not to years of paying mortgage interest and principal. After all, your most important priority is not buying anything you want, but attaining your mortgage goal.

As I mentioned above, the difference between need and want influences Kathy's and my gift giving practices. We do not purchase things for each other just because they are nice, even for special occasions.  Therefore, there are essentially no gifts for birthdays, anniversaries, Valentine's Day or Christmas/Hanukkah. We might go out for an informal dinner to celebrate, such as for a combined wedding anniversary (February 2nd) and Valentine's Day dinner.

This virtual lack of presents and buying items only when needed is actually positive. The practice may appear cruel, unusual, and a symptom of a problem marriage, but it's quite the opposite. The no-gift policy works well because it is based on a strong, loving relationship; we do not need to give gifts to prove anything. We know the priorities, we have our mindset, and we understand this practice is one of our tactics to accomplish our goals. Our no-gift program pays off (pun intended) for both of us.

My philosophy:  When you have a good and strong marriage, you do not need gifts.  When you have bad and weak marriage, no

amount of gifts will save the relationship.  Look at Hollywood.
The same philosophy applies to family and friends.

I admit the idea and custom of essentially no gifts takes some
getting used to for some individuals and couples. Please try it.
Confirm or discover you have a strong (or stronger than you
thought) relationship.  The marriage even improves when you work
and sacrifice together for the common goal and you both see the
benefits.

We purchase items and do things we need when we need
them—and can afford them. We don't wait for special occasions.
Establish the true need for purchasing something or doing something.  Then determine if you can afford to buy it or do it, at least at
that time.

## If You Can Not Afford It, Do Not Buy It

You know that you need to purchase something, but can you afford
it now?  By "afford it" I mean can you pay off the entire bill when
the statement arrives?  If you do not have the money to completely
pay off the bill that month, do not purchase the item that month.

Finance charges on the monthly unpaid balances of credit and
charge cards increases the price of each product or service you purchase.  The additional expense could be as much as eighteen to
twenty-one percent in unnecessary interest.

Do not buy anything using delayed debt.  The store says, "No
payment and no interest for six months."  First, delayed debt is still
debt.  You are trying hard to eliminate debt, not to defer it.  Second, read the fine print.  If you miss making the payment when
scheduled, even by one day, you are usually charged the full interest
that would have accumulated over the grace period. What a surprise!

Important:  Never have any unpaid balance and never have to
pay any finance charge or interest on a credit card or charge card—
none.

You may have to prioritize between two products that are
needed.  Purchase one item this month and the other next month.
Whatever it takes, you should be 100 percent debt-free at the end

of each month (except for a car loan [for a few months] and the mortgage, until it's paid-off).

The best way to have the money available for necessary purchases: maintain an appropriate budget and plan ahead. Know your monthly expenses and spending patterns. In addition to your income, maintain an adequate reserve to pay for expenses and spending. Establish a savings account for large, anticipated, and necessary spending (e.g., furniture, vacation, or a special project).

Whether you purchase a living room set or a trip to Disney World, when the bill comes, pay it in full. If you can't pay the bill in full at the end of the month, you can't afford the product (or vacation) at that time.

A living room set and a vacation are really discretionary spending, not basic necessities like electricity. Even though furniture or a trip are needed, you'll survive without them until you can afford it.

**Do Your Homework**

Whenever you buy something, no matter how inexpensive or very expensive the item, it's imperative to be a smart shopper. The more expensive the item, the more homework you need to do. Just as in school, doing your homework is not always fun at the time, but the effort pays off in the short run and long run. Use the many readily available resources.

Facilitate comparison shopping by checking the weekly circulars and ads in the daily newspaper for discount, department and specialty stores, supermarkets, or car dealerships.

When shopping for food or household products, know "the prices" and recognize what is and is not a good price for an item. Since you regularly shop for groceries, knowing the prices is relatively easy with your smart-shopper mindset.

As a smart shopper for expensive products, such as a stereo system or car, learn the prices and learn about (or know from experience) the product, manufacturer, and store. Telephone the store to answer questions about an advertised product and avoid unnecessary trips. Consider your own experience. If you have done well with a product, you're more likely to purchase another product from that manufacturer. The opposite is almost a certainty. When you have a negative experience, you're exceedingly unlikely to make the same mistake again. Ask family, friends, and neighbors about their experiences with a product, manufacturer, store, or dealer. Get specific information. Problem? Was it recent or one that occurred five years ago? How did the manufacturer, store, or dealership handle the situation? Resolving problems is important.

The local library is extremely useful. The library has general magazines and buyer's guides, such as Consumer Reports, that help you evaluate products in multiple categories. In addition, the library has specialty magazines on audio equipment, video products, computers, automobiles, and other specific groups. Since you make a major purchase once every few to many years, there is little need to subscribe to the specialty publications. These specialty magazines provide detailed reviews and analysis of products. Be aware of possible bias or patterns in reviews. Are the reviews always favorable? Remember the magazines (except Consumer Reports) are supported by manufacturers' advertising; evaluate the objectivity of the information. Look for other reviews in similar magazines and compare. The specialty magazines' ads help identify features you need and don't need. Have a note pad or clipboard handy and take notes, including the model numbers.

Comparison shopping takes time; consider it an investment. Go to the department or audio stores or car dealerships, with the clipboard. Take notes on the prices, model numbers, and important features. Get the names of the person(s) you speak with and a business card. Note the day, date and time you visited. Document the same information for all telephone conversations. These measures help avoid a "misunderstanding" and resolve problems in your favor. A big part of doing your homework is document, document, document.

Buying a car is probably the second most expensive purchase you make, after your house. Therefore, buying a car requires a ton of homework. Read reviews on the safety, reliability, comfort, economy, and resale of the vehicles you are considering. Call the local Better Business Bureau and Chamber of Commerce and ask if they have any record of complaints or compliments on file about the prospective dealers. Visit the service departments, observe, and ask car owners if they are satisfied with the service department. Test drive the cars you are considering. Buy a magazine that details what the dealer pays for options and what the same options cost on the stickers of new cars. Base your offer on the dealer's cost for the car and add two percent. (Be reasonable, the dealer has to make a profit to stay in business.) Or purchase a car, such as a Saturn or Oldsmobile, that has a manufacturer's fixed, no-dicker sticker price. The manufacturer has efficiently and economically built hundreds of thousands of cars with the same popular options. Therefore, the fixed price and value are reasonable. I avoid dealer fixed prices. Where is their economy of scale? Finally, take your time, shop around, avoid impulse actions, and be prepared to walk out if not completely satisfied with the transaction. They need you more than you need them.

For certain items, it's much more difficult to comparison shop. For example, one manufacturer may make a similar (but not identical) mattress for different stores with different model names. Get as much information as possible (e.g., on construction and content). You probably can't cut into the mattress to examine the construction of the product. The reputation of the store and the manufacturer's warranty may be all you have to go on (in addition to the price). It's not like buying a Snickers or Milky Way, when you know what your buying and can compare the candies.

## Avoid Purchasing Cheap Products and Services— Cheap Can be Expensive

It is usually best not to purchase the cheapest item among a group of similar products. This is especially true for higher priced products, for products with breakable mechanical parts, and for electronic components that are costly to repair or replace. When you spend a hundred, a thousand, or a few thousand dollars, there's a temptation to go with the cheapest option. But that could be an expensive mistake. You might think I would always be looking for the cheapest item to save the most money. True, I always want to save the most money—in the long run.

## Quality and Reliability

When you have a choice between a cheaper product and a more expensive product, evaluate their quality and reliability, consider their total, long-term costs, and select the one that is the best value. A large part of determining the value of a product is its quality and reliability. (The features and benefits of the product also help determine the value.) In general, the cheaper item is more likely to be of inferior or lesser quality and reliability than a more expensive item. Therefore, the cheaper item requires repairs or earlier replacement more often than the higher-priced alternative. Factor this into the total cost of the product. The more expensive item is frequently the best or better value.

Sometimes quality and reliability are reflected in the product's warranty or the manufacturer's reputation. These may or may not be dependable indicators. One important consideration is the history and future of the company. A 100-year warranty means nothing if the company goes out of business next week. Sears Craftsman hand tools, with their lifetime replacement warranty, are more expensive than many generic competitors. But the Craftsman hand tools are of obviously higher quality and they are replaced free if they ever break. And Sears should be in business for many years. Therefore, Craftsman hand tools are a better value than cheaper generic tools.

At times a good reputation is useless. I bought a compact disc player from a Japanese manufacturer with an excellent reputation for stereo components. I paid considerably more for the CD player than other, high quality, brand name players. I believed the wonderful reputation meant superior quality and reliability. It didn't. To make a long, aggravating story short, the CD player and the manufacturer were both lousy. All you can do is your best to get the best value. Usually it works, sometimes it doesn't.

It is possible a cheaper item and a more expensive item are approximately equal in quality and reliability. In that case, with all other factors being equal, the more expensive product is simply overpriced and not the best value. So buy the cheaper item and save money. There is a technical, financial term for paying a lot more money for one product and not getting a lot more value:  wasting your money.

Over the past twenty years, I've almost always been happy I purchased the higher quality and more reliable product over the cheaper or cheapest alternative. Also, when you buy a more expensive product on sale, you have a higher quality, more reliable product, perhaps for about the same price as the cheaper one at regular price. Greater quality and reliability means cost savings over time, less aggravation and headaches, and a better value.

Investment

Another example of cheap being expensive relates to "investment," such as with cars. Since you pay many thousands of dollars for a car, use brand name gasoline and properly maintain the vehicle. Consider the good gasoline and proper maintenance an investment in your car that pays off in the long run.

I believe cheap gasoline is more likely to be contaminated and, sooner or later, will foul the spark plugs and damage the engine. I wonder what's in the unmarked tanker trucks that deliver the gas to generic stations. There is always a possibility of problems with a brand name gas, but the risk is minimal and I expect some recourse with a large, reputable company. Save money by shopping around and pumping your own brand name gasoline, whenever possible.

Regular oil and filter changes, every 3,000 (to 6,000) miles, are essential for proper maintenance. You may think you can skip a few oil changes and save twenty to twenty-five dollars each. However, there's the possibility of engine damage from dirty oil or unrecognized oil loss, resulting in costly repairs, reduced value on resale, or both. Shop around for the best price on an oil and filter change from a reputable garage or dealer.

Think of painting or staining your house as an investment. Do you really want the painter who will do the job cheap? That is, a cheap job? The house is probably your biggest purchase, don't try to save a couple hundred dollars by hiring the cheapest painter and using cheap paint or stain. You would be reminded of the mistake every time you look at your home. Preparation (power wash, caulking seams, scraping flaking paint, and applying a priming coat) is as or more important than applying the finish coat of paint or stain. Properly maintaining your house is essential for appearance, avoiding costly repairs, and increasing the resale price. Do your homework and find a quality painter and paint or stain, not necessarily the most expensive and definitely not the cheapest. Do it yourself, only if you can do the job well.

It is good and financially wise to remember the saying, "Penny wise and pound foolish."

## Minimize Buying Convenience Products and Services— Convenience is Usually Costly

One of the necessary sacrifices in the mortgage war is doing without some conveniences. Convenience means you could do something yourself with more effort and time, but you pay a business to do it for you and spend money to save the effort and time. When a business provides a service or product that makes life easier, you pay higher prices and increase your spending. And when you increase spending on conveniences every day of every week of every month, year after year, that adds up to thousands and thousands of dollars that can go to winning the mortgage war.

Meals

Eliminate the increased spending on the convenience of dining out for breakfast, lunch, and/or dinner. Prepare your meals at home and decrease spending by many hundreds or thousands of dollars each year. You'll probably eat foods that are better for your health too.

What are your dining-out habits? Other than a breakfast business meeting and being on away on vacation, I can't think of one good reason to pay someone to make scrambled eggs. (Of course, when you're away on vacation scrambled eggs taste great.) I always took a wholesome lunch to work. I was never embarrassed and actually received some compliments for my healthy selections. People who went out for lunch every day talked about their salaries at least paying their mortgage. I thought, "What mortgage?" Sure, it's easy to go out for dinner. No preparation, everything is served, and no cleanup. Unless you are away from home (and the microwave, stove, and grill), please save going out for dinner for rare, extra-special occasions. Dining out morning, noon, and night is convenient—and expensive.

Eliminate the increased spending on the convenience of take-out meals from restaurants (primarily Chinese food and pizza) and supermarkets (salad bar, hot lasagna, or cooked chicken, etc.), and delivery (pizza). Perhaps you can prepare Chinese food and pizza from scratch at home. Otherwise, include these foods among your sacrifices for a greater cause. Prepare the supermarket take-out fare at home and save. If you buy take-out food for dinner only twice a week for about $25 or more each, that's about 100 meals and $2,500 or more in take-out spending each year. Remember, just as the spending adds up and up with take-out, the savings add up and up when you prepare your meals at home.

Also in the meals department, eliminate spending on prepared frozen dinners, breakfasts, and lunches. Unfortunately, many people pay a lot of money for the convenience of throwing a small amount of food in a microwave. How much did you spend on frozen dinners last year? You can buy a pound of boneless chicken breasts on sale for less than the price of a frozen chicken dinner with the meat portion about the size of your index finger, if you can find the meat at all.

Buy the boneless chicken on sale and grill or broil enough for your dinner plus some to freeze for future dinners. Use different sauces on different pieces. Then individually wrap each future dinner airtight in aluminum foil. Put a few servings in a gallon freezer bag, write the name of the item and date on a piece of scrap piece, and put the paper in the bag. For future dinners or lunches, just defrost a serving; preferably in the refrigerator, but room temperature or the microwave work too. Using the microwave, you can reheat the grilled chicken, bake potatoes, and prepare frozen vegetables for a nice dinner in about ten to fifteen minutes. Meatloaf and lasagna also work well with this system. How much money could you save by preparing your own meals and sacrificing the expensive convenience of frozen dinners and lunches?

Save with make-it-yourself breakfasts too. It's much less expensive to make a batch of waffles from scratch or use Bisquick (low fat [or regular] bought on sale with a coupon) than to buy frozen waffles. Home cooked waffles also taste better than factory frozen waffles. Prepare enough for both your current and several future breakfasts, as individual servings of homemade waffles (and pancakes) freeze well. Days and weeks later defrost and heat your waffles in the microwave, and then pop them in the toaster to get crispy, if desired.

If you absolutely, positively have to have some frozen dinners or breakfasts, please buy them only on sale and preferably with a coupon.

Never buy food or groceries in convenience stores. They are selling convenience and the price is astronomically high.

## Laundry

The commercial cleaner is another costly convenience. If a commercial laundry washes and presses your shirts, blouses, dresses, and other articles you increase your spending for convenience; although driving to and from the cleaners may not be convenient. How much do you spend at the commercial laundry? Buy a container of detergent on sale with a coupon, and do twelve loads of laundry for less than the price of having one shirt done at the cleaners. Significantly decrease your spending by doing your laundry (except dry cleaning, when required) at home.

## Shop At Home

Perhaps the most costly form of convenience is television home shopping. Eliminate it. Take the home shopping shows off the sequence channel selection of your remote, and cable box, if possible.

All the home shopping shows use several negative maneuvers to increase your spending. First, the convenience itself. It's too easy; just pick up the telephone and spend, spend, spend. Second, the clock ticking down and the limited number of items available increases the pressure to spend. Buy before you lose out on the "great deal." Third, spending is frequently based on impulse, not on your real need for the product. Please, never buy or spend on impulse. And fourth, you're at a disadvantage: you can't do your homework, examine the item, and comparison shop.

The "infomercial" products and services have negatives similar to television home shopping. Like unwelcome guests, the infomercials pop up at different times on different stations. Most are incredible, as in not credible. Many of the infomercials, especially the financial ones, add new meaning to the expression: "If it appears too good to be true, it probably is." Disregard the infomercials offers (forty-nine easy payments of $9.95) and save your hard earned money to pay off your mortgage.

Catalogs are another form of shop-at-home costly convenience. There isn't the pressure to buy now as with television home shopping and infomercials. However, the catalogs are always there, lying around, waiting for you to pick them up and order something. In addition, it is difficult to determine the real value of items and comparison shop, especially since all you have is a two dimensional representation. The dress is small and thin on a piece of paper. In most of the catalogs I've seen, the products seem expensive and poor values. Some catalog companies may substitute an item without your knowledge or approval. Or they add a tax to the purchase. Who pays for shipping when an item is returned? And as a bonus, once you order something from one catalog, you get a mailbox full of catalogs.

The only traditional catalog companies I have done well with are Jackson & Perkins Roses and Heartland Music. I know what I am buying, the products are guaranteed and a good value, and the companies stand behind their products and service.

Other Costly Conveniences

Think about your daily and weekly habits. Are you doing things and spending money for convenience, perhaps unintentionally, that you could do yourself and decrease spending?

You may not even consider money saving alternatives until you recognize the increased cost of convenience. For example, could you take public transportation and save on gasoline, tolls, parking, automobile insurance, and wear and tear on the car?

## Summary

You may be thinking, Ohmygod, I hardly have time to do everything I need or want to do now with many time-saving conveniences—how can I survive without them every day, day after day? It may be a difficult adjustment, but it is worth the effort. Focusing on your priorities—winning the mortgage war and enjoying the ultimate goal—helps a lot. Eliminate spending on costly and unnecessary conveniences.

Decreasing spending is a critical objective in the mortgage war. Every dollar you save by eliminating spending on conveniences adds up and can go to pay off the mortgage sooner.

## Always Think Value, Value, Value

It is essential to evaluate and determine the value of a product or service before you spend your money.

*The American Heritage College Dictionary*, 3rd ed. (Houghton Mifflin Co., 1993) defines value as "An amount, as of goods, services, or money, considered to be a fair and suitable equivalent for something else; a fair price or return."

My definition of value includes two crucial points. First, I evaluate and determine value based on the quality and quantity of a product or service at a good or excellent price for me, not just a "fair price." High quality in a product or service is important to me in assessing value and making comparisons. Quantity is usually easier to judge and compare. The good price for me almost always is a good sale or discount price; not just that the item is on sale.

The quality of a product is based on its parts, content (e.g., cotton vs. polyester) or ingredients, workmanship, and reliability; factors you can feel, see, hear, or smell or understand/know. Reliability is more implied than tangible. These factors relate to a product's "features and benefits."

Important: Always consider the "features and benefits" of a product or service. For example, a recliner has a leather seating area. The feature is leather. The benefits are leather wears well, does not stain, is easy to clean, and is comfortable. Another example, a car has anti-lock brakes (ABS). The feature is anti-lock brakes. The benefit is ABS, when used properly, help prevent skidding on wet or slippery roads. You pay for features and benefits.

Usually, more features means more expensive. Therefore, the big question to ask yourself: "Which specific features and benefits do I need, and which do I not need, when I buy a product or service?"

The second crucial point in my definition of value is that the product or service, even a high quality product or service at a good price, is worth it to me. Two questions arise. Does the product or service meet my current and anticipated needs, exceed my needs, or fail to meet my needs? And, can I afford the product or service? A new Rolls Royce for $150,000 is a high quality car at a relatively low, good price. Sounds like a great value. But the Rolls at $150,000 exceeds my needs and I can't afford it. The Rolls is not worth it to me. The product or service must be a good or great value to me.

Always remember to anticipate your needs as well as meet current needs. Don't buy a product that will be obsolete or clothing that will be too small before you get it home.

When you evaluate and compare the products and services you need to purchase always think value, value, value. A good or great value is a high quality product or service, in a good quantity, at a good or great price, that meets your current and anticipated needs, and is worth it to you.

### Patience Please—Buy Everything on a Good or Great Sale or Discount

When I say buy everything on sale, I do mean virtually everything. I look around my home and see almost everything, small or large, inexpensive or very expensive, was purchased on sale. Everything was bought not only on sale, but on a good or great sale or discount, at a good or great, low price. Getting a good or great sale or discount price may, and frequently does, require patience. Buying only on a good or great sale or discount is an important mindset and tactic to decrease spending.

Look around your home. What was purchased at a good sale or discount price? In my home (virtually) everything, from all towels, every wastebasket, each lamp, the light bulbs, and all window shades, to the living room set and big television, was bought on a good or great sale or discount. All clothing, from undershirts to suits, shoes and even the foam insoles were bought on sale. Most food and groceries were bought on sale, with a coupon, or both. With patience, it's almost always possible to buy high quality products at good or great sale prices.

An important tactic in buying everything on sale is knowing the types of stores that are best for the product or item you need. In addition, know the stores' patterns of having sales of different goods. Follow the ads and you'll see there are sales patterns for everything.

Always Take the Ad

Important: Always take the advertisement with you whenever and wherever you go shopping. Many times I shopped and the sale price was not posted or not posted correctly in the store. The salesperson was unaware of the sale or unaware of the correct sale price or percentage off. But, I always had the ad and could identify the model number or the specific garment on sale. Then the stores honored the advertised sale price without any problem . . . usually. Sometimes a discussion with a supervisor was necessary. Because I had the store's ad, disputes have always been resolved in my favor. To paraphrase Theodore Roosevelt: Speak nicely and carry a big ad.

Caution, always read the fine print in the ad, especially if you see an asterisk next to a price, with or without the words "original" price or "regular" price as the basis for the discount. The fine print may say something like: prices are offering prices which may or may not have caused real sales. In other words, the original or regular prices are basically inflated prices or suggested retail prices (that virtually nobody sells the product for), so the percentage off look greater. This is particularly a problem with some department stores.

The patience principle applies for whatever you need to purchase. I will discuss a couple of major categories.

Major Household Products

Specialty superstores have discount prices for a large selection of certain products, such as computers, stereos and televisions, toys, office supplies, pet supplies, and home goods and building supplies. These superstores are open to the public (vs. "warehouses" that require membership). They have low prices every day and sales for more savings. Shop around for the best price and most reputable store among similar superstores. In addition, discount and some department stores usually want to be competitive and may match the superstore's price, especially if you have the superstore's ad.

I never buy "used" or "reconditioned" anything that has any moving parts or electronic products, including cars. This essentially rules out purchasing anything used. Why buy a headache?

I do well buying appliances at discount stores and even a community appliance store that wants to be competitive and provides excellent service.

I usually buy linen, pillows, and towels at the department stores. By waiting for a great sale price, I get high quality, "famous maker" goods at an excellent price. If towels are seconds or irregulars; just check carefully before buying. Many times you can not find the irregularity. If there is a significant defect in a towel, buy a different one.

Reputable department stores are also a good source for furniture, mattresses and box springs, lamps, and rugs. They are (or should be) high quality products that last a long time. I wait until they are at great sale prices. If there's a problem, the large department stores, in business for decades, are very responsive. Do you know a reputable furniture store? Check their selection and sale prices against the department stores. Learn about the features and benefits of the sofa or dining room set, shop around, and compare bottom line sale prices (not just the percentage off ) before you buy. Then you know you really got a great sale price and value.

The membership discount warehouses usually require the purchase of huge quantities, which may be impractical. And the prices are not that great. I'm not favorably impressed with the big membership warehouses. I believe a smart, patient, comparison, value-focused shopper can do better at superstores and other stores than at membership warehouses.

Clothing and Accessories

For clothing, consider the season, what you need, and the type of store that best meets your needs. (We can rule out boutiques and specialty shops.) For clothing that changes with the seasons, such as pants, suits, dresses, and outerwear; generally you have two options: department stores and discount stores or "warehouses."

First, never buy clothes pre-season or in-season from a department store. Be patient; wait for the generous after-clearance sale. Avoid department stores with current season, first quality goods, as well as nice floors, escalators, friendly salespeople, and full retail prices. Ignore the newspaper or colorful circulars you get in the mail advertising clothing and accessories at full price or at the first, minimal sale price. The minimal sale price could be ten percent to twenty-five percent off the regular or retail price. Maybe some items are up to forty percent off the regular price. Ignore the second sale, twenty-five percent to forty percent off. Then comes the end-of-season clearance sale, perhaps up to fifty percent off. Sounds tempting. Do you buy then? Nooooo. Be patient. Wait for the after-clearance sale of, at the least, twenty-five percent off, up to forty percent off the clearance price, which is already fifty percent less than the retail price. The after-clearance sales savings is a wonderful sixty-three percent up to seventy percent off of the original retail price.

The math goes as follows. For example, the stated retail price of a dress is $100. Ignore every sale until preceded by the word "clearance." Then get ready, but don't buy. The clearance sale price is fifty percent off of $100 ($50 off). The dress now costs $50. The after-clearance sale is forty percent off of the clearance price of $50, an additional $20 off. That makes the $100 dress $30 or seventy percent off of the retail price. Buy now. The selection may not be as complete as three months earlier, but getting a $100 dress for $30 makes up for the heartbreak of reduced choices.

Reminder: Please review the above "caution" regarding the small print in ads and the stated regular or original prices. These prices may have been falsely increased on the tag, before the discounts. The bottom line price is more important than the percentage off. Therefore, always ask yourself, "Does the price make sense?"

Most important: How much does the item actually cost you and is the item a good or great value, as I defined above in "Always Think Value, Value, Value"?

The second and perhaps better option is the discount stores and "warehouses" (open to the public) that primarily feature off-price clothing, with other merchandise. These stores aren't as fancy as the department stores. But the discount stores and warehouses always have first quality (e.g., from overstocks or past season), seconds, or irregulars at a reduced, and sometimes good, price. In addition, they periodically have extra discounts or sales. The discount stores and warehouses also have clearance sales, but may not have after-clearance sales, for the seasonal items. I wait for the additional reductions.

For my undergarments, socks, and basic jeans I do best at general merchandise stores that also carry clothing. I buy on a good sale, of course. I usually don't buy any other articles of clothing at these stores.

Outlet stores may or may not have good prices and good values. For smart shopping, know two prices at an outlet: the usual retail price (which may not be the outlet's stated retail or list price) and the after-clearance sale price at a department or discount store. Outlet stores usually have a good selection, but they don't advertise specific garments. You may take a long drive and not find what you need. Often many outlet stores are together in a mall or area. Remember, buy only what you need and do not buy on impulse.

Supermarket Shopping (has its own chapter)

Bottom Lines

You spend thousands of your discretionary dollars each year buying many different things. Please have the spend-less-money mindset and buy everything—e-v-e-r-y-t-h-i-n-g—on a good or great sale or discount. At times this requires patience, which is rewarded. You save dimes, dollars, ten of dollars, or hundreds of dollars on each purchase. That adds up to thousands of dollars of savings and decreased spending every year; money that can go to pay off the mortgage early.

## Use VISA or MasterCard Whenever Possible (Really)

There are many benefits in making every purchase with a VISA or MasterCard. I have a VISA, so I use VISA in the discussion.

You probably think I'd say tear up, burn, and bury the ashes of your VISA, to avoid overcharging and getting in debt. However, we have the First and Second Purchasing Commandments, "Know the difference between need and want" and "If you can not afford it, do not buy it." I know you only make a purchase when you need the product or service and you pay off the entire bill when it comes. I'm not concerned about you abusing your VISA.

Rewards

Probably the biggest benefit from using VISA are the rewards you receive. The rewards come when you have a good VISA, an "affinity card," one that is affiliated with an airline, hotel, or automaker. These cards give you miles, points, or dollars that accumulate with each purchase. You should have a VISA issued through an airline, hotel or auto company.

I have a "Marriott Honored Guest Awards" VISA, issued as "First Card" by FCC National Bank. The "Honored Guest Awards" is Marriott's program for rewarding individuals who stay at Marriott hotels and resorts. In addition, Marriott offers a VISA to make purchases, including at their hotels, with bonus points. I always try to stay at a Marriott when I travel for business or pleasure. And I always use my Marriott VISA to make purchases everywhere, including groceries and gasoline. Therefore, I accumulate points both with hotel stays and VISA purchases. My Marriott VISA is the one and the only credit or charge card I use.

You might say, "Dave, what reward can you get by using your Marriott VISA?" Well, in 1991 I used most of the points I had accumulated, I chose the award, and I received paradise: ten nights at Marriott's Orlando World Center Resort Hotel, two round-trip airline tickets, and seven days' car rental—all free! I now have enough points to receive an award for at least seven nights at any Marriott resort or hotel in the world, two round-trip airline tickets, and seven days' car rental! Not bad.

You should have a VISA that rewards you. Every dollar charged on the VISA means more points (or airline miles or dollars toward the purchase of a car), and more points or miles, means more trips.

If you enroll in the Marriott Honored Guests Award program, request and fill out a Marriott First Card VISA application. If you have a good credit history and steady income, you are on your way to your dream vacation.

Again, I'm only talking about necessary purchases; not buying and charging things you don't need or can't pay for when the bill is due.

There's no good reason to have a VISA from a local or national bank, a gasoline company, or the Discover card. What do they do for you, especially compared with a Marriott, airline (such as American or Northwest Airlines), or automobile manufacturer (such as General Motors or Ford) VISA?

Use only the good, rewarding VISA. Don't use any store charge card, cash, or check. If the store, business, or service accepts VISA—use it. I do not charge anything less than $10 because of the fee the store has to pay to process the transaction.

Some people say you shouldn't charge something that will be gone before the bill comes, such as groceries or a meal. I say, "So what?" You pay for the groceries or meal anyway; so you may as well get points or miles toward a free trip.

Using your VISA has other benefits (check the Terms and Conditions of your card). First, if you're not satisfied with a product or service, and you have tried unsuccessfully to resolve the problem with the merchant, you can refuse to pay that portion of the VISA bill. This is strictly for 100% legitimate, significant problems and must be documented in writing. Second, if you rent a car, there's no need to purchase the optional insurance. You have insurance coverage when you charge the rental with your VISA. (In addition, your home owner's insurance may cover the car rental. Check your policy.) Third, if your card is lost or stolen, or the number is used illegally, your liability is limited. For example, your liability may be zero up to a maximum of fifty dollars.

The only benefits of a department or discount store charge card are the potential of a discount (e.g., ten percent) on your first purchase, rare special discount postcard notice or certificates, and receiving sales catalogs. For an especially large purchase, such as a living room set (on sale, of course), it's probably worth opening a charge for the additional ten percent off. The discount postcard notice or certificate may be useful; but make the purchase with VISA. Newspapers have the advertisement for sales, in black and white versus the color catalogs from the mailings.

Do not be concerned about the finance charge or interest rate on any unpaid balance for your good VISA. When you observe the Second Commandment of Purchasing, "If you can not afford it, do not buy it," you do not and will not ever have any finance charge to pay. I don't care if the finance charge is twenty-five percent. As I like to say, "I have never paid a darn dime in finance charges."

Pay your entire VISA bill by the due date, not the late charge date (when a finance charge accrues). Paying the entire bill on time, by the due date, every month does wonders for your credit rating.

Do not be concerned about the annual fee. True, you may find a bank with a lower or even no annual fee. But who cares? An annual fee of, for example, thirty-five dollars, is minuscule compared with the trips and vacations you receive.

The bottom line: Get a Marriott, airline, or automobile company VISA and use it for every purchase.

### Keep Accurate Records

Documenting your expenses and spending helps avoid or resolve billing disputes, and assists in managing finances and budgeting. Here is how I keep accurate records.

Spiral Notebook

I maintain my records in a spiral bound notebook. When opened, the two pages facing each other are used for one month. I write the month and year at the top of each page.

On the top half of the left page I document expenses: electricity, gas, telephone, cable TV,   and newspaper (on VISA).

On the right page I have three main columns.  On the left side I document grocery expenses, listing the store and VISA charge. In the middle column I write gasoline charges, listing the station and VISA charge. On the right side, I document spending and credits (in red), listing the store and the amount, usually on VISA.

On the lower half of each page, I document any additional expenses: real estate tax, excise tax, water bill, medical costs, home owner's insurance and stamps. I also document special spending, such as vacations, listing each VISA charge.

Receipts and Statements

I save all receipts and statements (some just temporarily) in a plastic box with alphabetical dividers.

All VISA receipts go under "V."  When the VISA bill arrives, I compare the merchant name and the amount of each purchase against my notebook record and check off both when they're correct. After I've confirmed that the supermarket, gasoline, and some store charges are billed correctly I discard those receipts, tearing them into little pieces.

I keep the receipts for larger purchases.  For special items (e.g., the stereo system, computer, and lawn tractor), I have a ten inch by thirteen inch envelope for each item to keep the receipts, product information, manual, warranty information, and related documents. The envelopes are kept together in a filing cabinet for easy reference.

Always check off your VISA bill, item by item and amount by amount, including credits, against the notebook entries. If there's an error, you have the receipt to document the correct amount. Also, make sure you are credited for the credits; double-check the notebook, looking for credits. If you find a credit, check the VISA statement. If you did not get a credit, it may appear next month.  I save all VISA statements.

One month I was going down the VISA statement, checking each item off, and—oh boy—I found two airline "tickets-by-mail" charged to my account.  Unfortunately, I wasn't going anywhere at the time and I hadn't purchased the tickets. I followed the appropriate procedure, immediately called VISA, and I was not responsible for those illegal charges. The account was immediately terminated and I received a new account number and cards within a couple days. I tried to provide information to help VISA track down the criminal. Even if you are careful with your card and it is not stolen or lost, there is always the risk of criminal activity from routine charges. Sickeningly, criminal activity results in higher costs of goods and services for everyone.

Important: Never give your credit card (or checking or savings) account number over the telephone to anyone who calls you, unless you know the individual personally. Also, be extremely careful disposing of receipts or documents with your account number on them. Rip the papers into many pieces. Criminals go through trash to get account numbers and names.

On the portion of the monthly utility bills I keep, I write the check number and the date I paid the bill. I file the new statement in the receipt box and discard the old statement, after confirming that the previous payment was properly credited to my account. I rip up all statements.

Managing Finances and Budgeting

Documenting all your expenses and spending in the notebook also helps you to manage your finances. First, you need to know how much money is going out each month and where the money is going. Then, the big question: Where will you reduce expenses and spending? The big answer: Everywhere! Use the tactics to reduce expenses and spending and you have documented proof of your progress for positive reinforcement.

Decreased expenses and spending enables you to successfully budget and try to live on one income; especially TINKs (two incomes and no kids). The second income goes exclusively to pay off (or save for) the mortgage. Even if you have only one income, reducing expenses and spending increases the amount of money that can go to win the mortgage war.

For those have a deficit (you spend more than you take home in earnings) each month and an increasing total debt (your monthly deficits are added on top of previous deficits), documenting your expenses and spending is crucial. Why and where are you out of control? You have to see, in an organized, complete way, what you're doing to yourself. Then establish your priorities and mindset, and take control of your spending habits and finances. Use the tactics discussed in this and other chapters to establish new, responsible, and better spending practices, and pay off your bills. After you pay off all of your credit card and other monthly debts, begin to pay extra to principal (ETP) and pay off your mortgage early (and car loan, if applicable). First things first.

## Children

Although I don't have any children, I believe the spend-less-money mindset applies to spending on your children and benefits your children in three ways. One, your spend-less-money mindset and the necessary tactics you use demonstrate every day by parental example: need versus want, self-discipline, patience, value, sacrifice, and others, and their rewards. These examples are valuable lessons for children in a time when "I want . . . " and a flood of consumer goods may warp children's expectations. Two, fewer objects to keep children occupied can result in more time for family activities. And three, mortgage victory benefits the entire family, including the children's future.

## Summary

Whatever your income and financial status, observe the Nine Commandments of Purchasing tactics on a daily basis, week after week, after month, after year. You will have more money to win the mortgage battle every month with large ETP payments and win the mortgage war years ahead of schedule. Your ultimate goal is attainable. It's all up to you.

Now, what are the Nine Commandments of Purchasing?

Just in case you could not remember one of them, here they are:

## The Nine Commandments of Purchasing

Know the Difference between Need and Want

If You Can Not Afford It, Do Not Buy It

Do Your Homework

Avoid Purchasing Cheap Products and Services—Cheap Can Be Expensive

Minimize Buying Convenience Goods and Services—Convenience Is Usually Costly

Always Think Value, Value, Value

Patience Please—Buy Everything on a Good or Great Sale or Good Discount

Use VISA or MasterCard Whenever Possible (Really)

Keep Accurate Records


## Bonus Commandment

## Do Not Give Your Money Away to Fraud—Be Smart and Use Common Sense

Sadly, money is given away to thieves every day, not angrily at the point of a gun, but willingly through fraud. Successful fraud usually depends on you being greedy or charitable.

Greed is thinking you can get something for nothing, or next to nothing. Whether by telephone or mail, when notified that you have won a prize for a contest you never entered:  hang up the phone (politely) or rip up the mail, respectively. Don't wait for the line, "all you need to do to get the prize is give me your credit card number" or see "to receive the prize just send a check . . . . " Use your common-sense reflexes: "Congratulations, you have won a prize"—hang up or tear up. Period.

Never give your credit card number, checking account number, social security number, or any financial information to anyone that *calls you* or *writes to you*, unless you know the individual personally (or organization very well and verify, if you have any questions). That goes for cash too.

Know who you're doing business with. A guy comes up to you outside ABCD department store. He says ABCD is having a special today: $100 for a new nineteen-inch color television. Just give him the cash and go around back to the loading dock to pick up the set. Oh boy! A color TV for $100. What a bargain. The guy and your $100 are gone by the time you reach the loading dock, where they don't know what you're talking about.

Some fraud is more deceptive or misleading, rather than outright theft. You get a letter with big print saying you have won a "free trip." The small print, at the bottom of the last page says something like: accommodations are provided by FleaBag International, the prize does not include air fare, ground transportation, meals, taxes, tips, or anything else, including an upgrade to a decent hotel. You learn about the details after you have paid your nonrefundable deposit. Again, the trip is really not something for nothing, it's nothing for something. Use common sense; avoid greed.

Unfortunately, charity fraud takes advantage of the most good-hearted people. The supposed charity may have a name that sounds official similar to a reputable charity. You are more likely to listen on the telephone or read a letter about a charity, than winning a nonexistent prize. As soon as you are asked for your credit card number — reflex—terminate the discussion.

Be charitable and smart, give to causes you know are reputable and use your donation wisely. Ask how much of donations actually go to good works (e.g. research, medical care, helping animals) rather than administration.

Get a receipt for your donation. You give because you're helping a charity, but use the federal income tax deduction, and you can give more next year. Also, a reputable charity provides a receipt, a fraudulent group is much less likely to give you anything in writing. Although, something in writing is no guarantee of legitimacy.

Other forms of fraud exist. For example, you hire someone for a project, give him a deposit, and he never shows up or he does not finish the work. Did you get and check references? Do you have a receipt for the deposit and a written agreement specifying the work to be done and a timetable? Yes. Well, you did your best and have some legal recourse.

Be smart, use common sense not greed, and you have more money to donate and pay off the mortgage.

I guess there really are ten commandments.

# Chapter 7

# Save Money with Smart Supermarket Shopping

Many tactics reduce the expense of food and other groceries, and save a lot of money in the supermarket. You are probably there more often and make more purchases in the supermarket than any other setting.

How much do you spend on groceries in a year? Even for just two people, you probably spend a few thousand of dollars annually. In addition to observing the "Nine Commandments of Purchasing," you save at least two thousand dollars a year by using the Six Supermarket Savings Steps.

**Six Supermarket Savings Steps**

Know Your Prices

Establish a Strict Price Threshold

Buy on a Good or Great Sale and(or) Use Coupons

Avoid Brand Loyalty

Use Simple Math

Pay Attention, Especially at Checkout

**Know Your Prices**

You shop regularly, so you should be familiar with the prices of the items you need and buy. Don't just take items off the shelves and meat out of the case and throw them in the basket. Pay attention to prices and save a ton of money.

You have to know your prices—what is a good price and what is not a good price—for all  the groceries you buy. It's easy and second nature.  Honest.

**Establish a Strict Price Threshold**

When you know your prices, you can establish a strict threshold for the maximum you spend for all items; a threshold price mindset. It doesn't matter what the item: meat, produce, dairy, cookies, or laundry detergent. Determine the highest price you pay for every food or household product, and stick to it. This price is usually a good sale price for the item. The threshold price may only be available once a month (for one week) in a store.

Threshold prices may vary somewhat by region of the country. However, for you, the threshold prices are constant throughout the year. There may be times of the year when certain produce is readily available at or below your threshold price. Great. At other times, fruits or vegetables are available, but at greater than your threshold price. Remember your threshold price mindset, and do without the item.

For example, the most I pay for a head of iceberg or any other lettuce is $.99. If lettuce is less than a dollar, as it is frequently during the summer, then I buy lettuce if I need it. If lettuce is more than one dollar, either $1.09 or up to $1.99, it doesn't matter if I don't have any lettuce, I will not buy it. I may go for a few weeks without iceberg lettuce. Perhaps another type of lettuce, such as green leaf, red leaf, romaine, or Boston, is $.99 or less. If so, I have an alternative. If not, I go without lettuce. There are plenty of other vegetables.

As another example, the most I pay for boneless, center cut pork chops is $2.99 per pound, well below the usual price range of $4.69 to 5.49 a pound.  No boneless pork chops at or below my threshold price?  I eat something else. That's part of the threshold mindset and a small sacrifice.

Important: I always purchase high quality, excellent cuts of meat; but only at or below my threshold price for those cuts. For instance, I buy only choice grade boneless sirloin strip steaks, filet mignon, ground sirloin (fifteen percent fat) hamburger, and london broil; center cut pork chops, rib or loin lamb chops, and chicken breasts. A well-known steak restaurant has a butcher shop with excellent meats, especially beef, and weekly sales.  It is a long drive to get there, but when they have the right meats at the right prices, it's worth the ride. And I stock up. This butcher shop is a great supplement to the supermarkets' meats. With threshold prices, it is not necessary to, and you should not, sacrifice quality in meats. In fact, you may eat better than you do now, for less money.

The threshold principle applies to all categories of food and household products. The limits are set. These limits are adjusted gradually for inflation—only. Some threshold prices may last for several years. My record:  I still pay ninety-nine cents per pound for whole or split chicken breasts, as I did fifteen years ago. Even with strict threshold prices, I have not missed a meal and I remain well nourished.

**Buy on a Good or Great Sale and(or) with Coupons**

Buying food and household products when they are on good or great sales and you have a coupon for the items is shopping bliss. The next best thing is for the items to be on a good sale or you have a coupon for the product. Any way, you want items at or below your threshold price.

Buy On a Good or Great Sale

The weekly supermarket circulars/advertisements are essential for smart shopping. Please remember, with our constitutional right of free speech, an item may be in an ad and not actually be selling for much or any less than the usual price.

At home, go through the circulars looking for products you use and are on sale at or below your threshold price—a good or great sale. Circle or mark those items.

The three questions

After you mark the circulars, there are usually three questions to ask yourself.

1.  Do I need this item now or this week?

2.  Am I low on the item (running out with no backup or alternative)?

If the answer is "yes" to either question, when you go to the store, first see if you have any coupons for the product. If you usually have coupons, but don't have any coupons at the time, purchase only one of the item. If you rarely or never have any coupons for the product, purchase a couple, few or several of the product, depending on how long it lasts, how often you use it up, and what you need for reserve.

3.  Will I use the product eventually (could I use it as backup)?

If so, when you go to the store, see if you have one or more coupons for the product. Only purchase as much of the product as you have coupons for.

Important reminders

Please remember, each supermarket usually has at least one national brand product in each category, such as laundry detergent or cheese, on sale each week. These are featured on the front of the circular, with the specific section, such as household or dairy, or both.

In addition, most specific products (e.g., Fab laundry detergent or Kraft Cracker Barrel cheese) are on sale in a particular supermarket about every four weeks.

Some sale prices are better than others. Sale prices may or may not be "good sale prices," at or below your threshold price for the products.

Each time you shop, have a shopping list of the items you need in addition to the marked ads.

You may need to get and use a store card for the sale prices. I don't care if the store is monitoring shopping habits. Use the card every time you shop.

### The two supermarket approach

If possible, shop at two supermarkets; increase your chances that you need are on sale at or below your threshold price. When you regularly shop at two stores you get to know the layout of the stores and  increase your shopping efficiency .

I shop at two stores that are clean, well stocked, efficient, have nice staff and are, fortunately, close to each other. The supermarkets are about twenty minutes away from my house.

I avoid going to a store that is five minutes away and drive by another on the way to the two supermarkets. These stores are backups only, and used reluctantly.  I avoid these latter two stores primarily because the help are either not friendly (on a good day) or rude, rarely helpful, and smile and say "thank you" as often as the sun sets in the east. Grocery shopping may not be like going to Disney World, but it should not be a dreaded, aggravating experience.

I find the supermarket superstores usually too large (a golf cart would help to get around), and their circulars cluttered with too many items.

Always take both circulars into each store. That way, if you consider buying an item in one store (perhaps an unadvertised special for that store), you can quickly check the sale prices in the other store and you don't have to trust your memory. Be aware one store may have a display for a product that is not on sale in that store.  The item is on sale at a competitor. Coincidence?  Perhaps. But don't be fooled.  Also, just because there is a huge display does not necessarily mean that there is good sale.

Always keep your eyes open for unadvertised sales or price reductions by the store or manufacturer. These may appear on shelf tags or as bright stickers on the package. The fifty percent off day-old, in-store bakery breads, muffins, and pastries (usually on a special rack) is a good example of a great price reduction.

Also, look for "bonus size," "get an extra six ounces frees," "buy one / get one free," and similar manufacturer or store offers. They are usually available at the regular, and sometimes even the sale, price. Be careful, some buy one at the regular price and get one free offers are more expensive than buying one (or two) on sale (i.e., the sale price may be more than fifty percent off the regular price).

Sometimes supermarkets have store coupons in their circulars. These coupons just limit the number of items available at the sale price. At the register, you are charged the regular price, then the store coupon is used to deduct an amount to bring that item down to the advertised sale price. You can use a manufacturer's coupon too.

## Coupons

Clipping, organizing, storing and using coupons is well worth the effort. Coupons will save you several hundred dollars a year. There are a few things to keep in mind to make using coupons easy.

### Clipping coupons

The best source of coupons is inserts in the Sunday newspaper. The savings from coupons more than makes up for the cost of the newspaper. (In addition, with the television guide from the Sunday paper you never have to buy *TV Guide*.) Coupons are also available in the newspaper's food section and coupon bulk mailings.

Save time and storage space by only cutting out coupons for those products you know you will or could buy sooner or later. Keeping unnecessary coupons only increases the time to file the coupons, increases the weight of the coupons, and increases the time to find the ones you want. I file new coupons about once a week, depending on how many I clip at a time.

Many national brand manufacturers have coupons on a regular basis. Therefore, you may have two or more coupons for a product. That's wonderful. In the world of coupons duplicate or triplicate is good. You can stock up on some items. Also, when one coupon expires you still have another. If you will or could buy the product, keep all the coupons you find.

Supermarkets may have sales on certain items to coordinate with coupons in the Sunday newspaper. Cut out all your coupons before you shop each week. Even if you don't get a chance to file them, at least you have the coupons with you.

## Organizing and storing coupons

To organize and store the coupons, I use a covered cardboard box (six inches by five inches by eleven inches) with alphabetical dividers. The box fits nicely in the child seat of the carriage (if there is no child). Some people use an accordion file. Use whatever works best for you.

I file many coupons individually by brand name, such as Arnold breads, All laundry detergent, and A1 steak sauce under "A." If I have more than one coupon for a product I keep them together, with the highest valued ones in front. I also file coupons by group for certain companies with several product lines, such as Pillsbury, Kraft, and Lysol. Within each letter section, I place the coupons I use most frequently toward the front for convenience. An alternative approach is to organize by types of products; all detergents or all cookies are kept together alphabetically within each group.

Most coupons expire on the last date of a month. At the end of each month I remove the expired coupons and file the newest batch. It takes me a total of about an hour a month to maintain the coupon system. Clipping coupons does not require absolute concentration; I do it while watching TV or listening to music. If you are just starting, it will probably take you more time to collect and organize the coupons and a couple of months to accumulate a good supply.

## Using coupons

Shop at supermarkets that always double the value of manufacturer's coupons, if possible. Usually this applies to coupons with a face value of up to ninety-nine cents. If the total value of the coupon when doubled exceeds the price of the item, you get the item free. That's hard to beat. Sometimes there's a maximum of one dollar credit.

Some stores do not double coupons. These stores claim their regular prices are less than the regular prices of stores that do double coupons. I'm not convinced. More important, I buy most items on sale anyway.

Some supermarkets have store coupons in their circulars that allow a certain number of manufacturers' coupons to be tripled, in addition to all other coupons being doubled. Terrific. That's especially useful for high value coupons. The triple coupons help to get items below your threshold price and increase the chances of getting some items free.

Always bring all of your coupons with you each time you shop. It's easy to bring the whole bunch. And it's good to have all your coupons available just in case you find unanticipated bargains, such as unadvertised specials and in-store or manufacturer's sales.

Pay attention to restrictions on coupons. A coupon may be valid only with the purchase of a particular size or specific variety or flavor of the product. The best coupons say "any size and variety."

There are several types of products, such as laundry detergent, hand/bath soap, dishwasher detergent, and household cleaners, that you only (always) buy with a coupon(s) to be doubled and on a good sale. Buy sufficient quantities so you never run out and never have to buy the item without a coupon and at regular price. That would be a supermarket sin. For many other items, you usually (vs. always) buy with a coupon(s) to be doubled and on a good sale.

As you shop and select coupons you use, put them in an empty jacket or pants pocket or a separate area until checkout. Give them to the cashier before the scanning begins. You may forget them if you wait until the end. Double check to make sure you have taken all of the coupons out of your pocket.

Summary

It helps when you get immediate positive feedback that your efforts to buy on a good or great sale and use coupons are paying off, literally. If there's a subtotal before the coupons are scanned or credited, you see the specific savings from the doubled coupons. Whether you calculate the percentage saved from the total amount or the actual dollars saved (which is more important), the doubled coupons make a big difference. Keep in mind, if you paid for the coupon items separately (did not include meat, produce, and items you did not use a coupon for), you would really appreciate the stupendous savings with coupons.

Unfortunately, most supermarkets don't document on the receipt how much you saved by buying items on sale versus the regular price. Therefore, it's not easy to see the amount you saved by being a smart and patient shopper. But you know in your heart the savings is substantial. If you bought five pounds of boneless and skinless chicken breasts for $1.99 per pound rather than the regular price of $3.49 a pound, you saved $7.50 right there.

The savings from coupons and buying on a good or great sale are cumulative, every week, month after month; adding up to thousands of dollars.

## Avoid Brand Loyalty

I usually do not have any specific "brand loyalty."  I'm looking for whatever the item is I need; preferably as one of the brand name products, at or below my threshold price, and I have a coupon for the product.

Here are some examples. I use any brand name laundry detergent. They all do a good job. The laundry detergent I buy is the one on sale at my threshold price of $1.99 or less for thirty-two ounce "Ultra" (or the equivalent) and I have a coupon for (which is doubled, usually to $1). I purchase any brand name premium, "not from concentrate," orange juice. I only buy the premium because the premium products are far superior to the "made from concentrate" alternatives.  My threshold price for the premium O.J. is $1.99 for a half gallon on sale, and I usually get it for $1.79 or less. I have a coupon to further reduce the price about half of the time. I buy the premium product for about the same amount as the regular price for "made from concentrate" juices.

I have some brand preferences. Among the premium O.J. products, I prefer the Tropicana Grovestand. The Grovestand really does taste like fresh squeezed. When the Grovestand is $1.79 or less I get at least two half gallons, with or without coupons. If I run out of Grovestand and another premium O.J. is on sale at a good price I get one, with or without a coupon. If I have more than one coupon I buy as many of the alternative products as I have a coupon for. Grovestand is an example of a brand preference, not brand loyalty.

I have a brand loyalty only when products demonstrate features and benefits superior to the competition. These products have a greater value, even if they are more expensive than competitors.

For me, Edge gel works far better than anything else I have used for shaving. Before I tried Edge, at times I looked like I shaved while blindfolded, using a rusty machete. Less expensive shaving creams and other gels are available. However, I remain loyal to Edge. I only buy it on a good sale, with a coupon; so I get the lowest price possible.

The Gillette Sensor razor is another example of a product for which I have a brand loyalty based on value. The Sensor razor and the Edge gel work great together. When I first bought the Sensor razor, Gillette said their Foamy shaving cream worked best with the their razor. I was skeptical. But the razor was wonderful; so Gillette had some credibility. Therefore, even though I loved the Edge gel, I bought and tried the Gillette Foamy shaving cream. The Foamy did not work nearly as well as the Edge and I'll never purchase Foamy again. The lesson I learned: One may buy a product or service for the first time in good faith based on a good reason; but the merits of the product or service itself is the only reason you ever buy it again.

I do have some "brand disloyalty." If I don't like a product, I don't save coupons for it and I don't buy it, even if it is on sale. For instance, I tried a brand name Vegetable Beef soup when it was new. There were huge savings with the sale price and coupons to "launch" the new product line of soups. The big problem: I could not positively identify any solid substance that was not a vegetable, as being a meat, let alone beef. I called the company and explained the puzzling situation. They were nice and sent me a coupon for a free can. Open minded, I tried it again—with the same results. I will not buy any more of their "soups" or any of their other products.

Store Brands

Store brands can be good, high quality, economical alternatives to national brand name products. The store brands may even have been prepared by a national brand manufacturer to the specifications of the supermarket chain. The regular price for products with the store's name on the label is usually less than the regular price of the equivalent brand name product. And the store brand may also go on sale periodically.

Unfortunately, store brand items do not have manufacturer's coupons. National brand products at a good sale price are usually less expensive than the regular price of the equivalent store brand product, especially when you also have a doubled manufacturer's coupon. When I can buy a national brand item for less than a store brand, I always purchase the national brand product. Store brands are an alternative for certain items, such as some frozen vegetables, ice cream, and apple sauce.

Store brands are higher quality than generic products (the old white package with the black lettering). I don't purchase generic groceries; they aren't worth their cheap price.

**Use Simple Math**

At times you need to compare two different sizes and prices of a product, or compare two competitive products, to determine the most economical—the best price per unit (e.g., ounce [weight or volume] or 100). You usually do not need a calculator to decide the best buy.

First Example

Crisis: You need a product that is not on sale anywhere, you can not use a similar product that is on sale or the store brand as an alternative, and you do not have a coupon! Fortunately, you know which store has the product at the lowest regular price and you go there.

The product is a liquid that comes in two sizes, eight ounces for $1.29 and sixteen ounces for $1.99. The shelf marker should give you the unit price. This is 16.1 cents per ounce for the smaller bottle and 12.4 cents per ounce for the larger bottle. If you can use the larger amount, the sixteen ounce size is the most economical, saving you about four cents per ounce. If you only need two ounces and will never use the product again or it will expire before you are likely to need it again, buy the smaller size and save seventy cents.

Second Example

Important: When you use a coupon, always calculate the after-coupon, net price to compare the cost of two items. Contrary to a popular impression, that the larger size is always the most economical, when using a coupon, the smallest size may be, and frequently is, the least expensive per unit. This is especially true when higher-valued coupons are doubled.

You have a $.50 coupon for any size of the product from the First Example. The supermarket doubles the value of your $.50 coupon to equal $1. The cost of the sixteen ounce bottle is $1.99 minus $1 equals $.99 (call it a dollar). The cost of the eight ounce bottle is $1.29 minus $1 equals only $.29 cents (call it $.30).

Which size is the best buy with the doubled coupon? It's simple to determine which size has the lowest after-coupon, net price when comparing sizes or numbers that are easy proportions of each other (eight and sixteen ounces, 50 or 100 whatevers, a pint and a quart). To evaluate, just double the after-coupon, net price of the smaller size and compare that amount to the after-coupon, net price of the larger size.

In this example, double the $.30 for the eight ounces and you have $.60 for (per) sixteen ounces versus the sixteen ounce bottle for a dollar, as the after-coupon, net prices. The small size is the best value when using the doubled $.50 coupon. What if the coupon is for $.60, to be doubled? The eight ounce bottle now costs $.09 ($1.29 - $1.20) versus the sixteen ounce bottle costing $.79 ($1.99 - $1.20). For comparison, double the nine cents for the eight ounce bottle to $.18 per sixteen ounces versus the sixteen ounce bottle for $.79 cents, as the after-coupon, net prices. If the coupon is for $.65, the eight ounce bottle is free! In this example, and in many other situations, the small size is the most economical with a doubled coupon.

## Third Example

Even determining the lowest after-coupon, net price of sizes with slightly more complicated proportions, say twelve and eighteen ounce bottles, is easy. To evaluate, just figure the after-coupon, net price of the twelve ounce size and add one-half of that amount to the after-coupon, net price of the twelve ounce bottle (for the equivalent of eighteen ounces). Compare that price to the after-coupon, net price of the eighteen ounce bottle.

Translated example:  The shelf prices of the twelve and eighteen ounce bottles are  $1.99 and $2.99, respectively. Your coupon is for $.50, to be doubled. Therefore, the after-coupon, net price of the twelve ounce bottle is $1, rounded off. The eighteen ounce bottle is $2, rounded off.  To evaluate: For the twelve ounce bottle, just take $1 for twelve ounces and add one-half of $1, equals $1.50 per eighteen ounces. Compare that to the eighteen ounce bottle for $2. Again, the smaller size is the better buy, with the lower after-coupon, net price.

## Pay Attention, Especially at Checkout

Any time human beings price an item or program a computer for the register, there's potential for error. You make too big an effort to decrease food expenses with your strict threshold prices and coupons to have errors negate your savings. Therefore, pay attention, particularly at certain times.

Deli, Etc.

In the deli, meat, and produce departments, always check to make sure the price per pound and the weight on the package are what you expect them to be. In the deli department, after the meat or cheese is weighed, a code is entered to produce the tag that goes on the package. If the deli person hits the wrong buttons, you get the wrong price.  It has happened to me.  I expect the sale price for the sliced turkey and a different, higher price per pound is used (for a different type of turkey). If I didn't check, I probably wouldn't notice it.

The same goes for the meat case. When meats are packaged, the price per pound may be entered incorrectly in the system and the meat that is supposed to be on sale is labeled with a higher price per pound and total price. Rarely, the weight is off and obviously does not make sense. Check to see that the weight seems correct too (you don't need a scale).

Some produce (such as grapes) may be prepackaged and priced. Confirm that the price per pound and weight (approximately) are correct.

Unit Price

The unit price on the shelf tags can be wrong. When you compare unit prices you need the correct unit price for each product and size. The unit price may be based on an old price, the unit price may be based on the regular price when the item is actually on sale, or the unit price may be just plain wrong. A quick check to make sure the unit price seems right (does it make sense?) is easy and useful. Also, when comparing two sizes of one product, the unit prices may be based on a different amounts (e.g., per ounce and per pound); make sure you compare "apples to apples."

Checkout

Most errors occur at checkout during the rapid-fire scanning. Ideally, if two people can shop together, at checkout one person can put the groceries on the belt and the other can watch the cash register display screen as the items and prices appear when the groceries are scanned. Some supermarkets have carts that allow the cashier to remove the items. This allows you to shop alone and still watch the screen.

There are direct and indirect human errors. The cashier may enter the wrong code for loose, pick-your-own produce and you get charged the wrong price per pound. One time I saw "organic tomatoes" on the screen when my sweet potatoes were being weighed and going through. There was quite a difference in the prices per pound and the final prices.

The biggest problem occurs when the wrong price is in the computer for an item, especially an item on sale. That item is scanned and you are automatically charged the wrong, usually higher, price. Everything is scanned so quickly you really have to pay close attention. It's difficult for one person to unload the shopping cart and watch the screen at the same time. In order to catch and point out an error, you have to know the correct price. You may have to show the ad with the sale price or the item with the price sticker to the cashier. At one supermarket, if they charge more for an item than the price should be, I get the item free. If I purchased more than one of the product, I get one free and the others at the lower, correct price.

Also watch as the coupons are scanned. Coupons can stick together and be overlooked, or they may be forgotten. A friendly reminder to the cashier ensures you get the savings you deserve.

**Additional Helpful Hints**

Always check the "use by," "best to buy by," or "expiration date" on any and all dated products. Not only to make sure you will use (or freeze, if appropriate) the product by the date, but also to assure you're buying the freshest item available. This applies to anything in the dairy case (milk, canned whipped cream, cheeses, yogurt, orange juice, or refrigerated pickles), baked goods, packaged meats (supermarket or national brands), salad dressings, mayonnaise, ice cream, and many other items.

Please read the Nutrition Facts labels. They are extremely informative and help you make wise choices.

For your health and well-being (physical and financial [indirectly]), please try the "reduced fat," "low fat," and, preferably, "fat free" products. The quality, in taste, smell, sight, texture, and selection have improved tremendously over the past few years. "Reduced fat" is a comparison with the regular form of the product or a competitor's product. For example, fifty percent less, thirty-three percent less, or twenty-five percent less fat than a competitor's or the regular form of the cookie or cracker. "Low fat" means the amount of fat in the item is at or below a certain standard. "Fat free" means there's no fat in a serving size of the product. Pay attention to the serving sizes, they may be unusually or unrealistically small. These reduced fat, low fat or fat free products are not usually free of calories. In fact, sugar may somewhat make up for the taste changes from the fat reduction or elimination. Therefore, do not think you can eat as many cookies as you like and avoid the calories just because the cookie is fat free. That could be a big, fat mistake! The amount (in grams [g]) and the percentage of the calories from fat is also important. The lower the better. A total of sixty-five grams of fat or less (ideally) and less than thirty percent of calories from fat are preferable for the total diet each day.

Even fat free, otherwise known as skim, milk tastes good. If you are accustomed to whole milk (which is four percent fat), you may have to taper down to skim. First try the two percent for a gallon or two. Two percent still has half of the fat of whole milk. Then the one percent for a couple of gallons. And finally switch to the skim, nonfat milk. You get all of the nutrients, calcium, and protein from the milk (just like whole), but you don't get the fat, which you (and your children, if applicable) probably do not need anyway. After you drink skim milk for a while, whole milk tastes funny, like a glass of heavy cream.

When buying meats, use a produce bag as a second package, especially for chicken, which can leak. Use one plastic bag for each package of meat and have the clear side of the plastic bag over the price label so the meat can be scanned easily. The extra bag is also good at home for added freshness protection and to avoid leaks in the refrigerator and on the kitchen floor.

In order to preserve the natural color, smell, texture, and taste of fresh meats and prevent bacterial growth and spoilage, freeze all meat (especially beef and chicken) as soon as possible; preferably the same day or the day after you bought it. Trim all fat off the meat before freezing. It seems easier to get rid of the fat sooner than later. The meat needs less aluminum foil to wrap and takes up less room in the freezer. When you have several steaks and chops to freeze, you see how much room you save by not freezing fat. Defrosting the meat in the microwave, if necessary, is easier without the fat.

When unloading your cart in the supermarket, first put out the heavier items, such as household products and soda/pop/tonic bottles or cans, then any paper goods, then packaged foods, then frozen foods, then meats, and finally the things that can get crushed, such as leaf lettuce (e.g., Boston), certain delicate fruits (e.g., raspberries), bread, and bakery items. The frozen foods should be bagged separately to keep them cold and avoid condensation on other items. The meats can go with the frozen foods to keep the meats cold or be bagged separately.

### Summary

You spend thousands of dollars in the supermarket each year. Please look at the Six Supermarket Savings Steps as tactics to drastically decrease the expense of food, and still eat as well or better than you do now. When you use all the tactics, you can easily save at least $40 a week on average, that's over $2,000 a year. You really should save much more. Whatever you save in food expenses goes to win the mortgage war.

Here they are again, the Six Supermarket Savings Steps:

Know Your Prices

Establish a Strict Price Threshold

Buy on a Good or Great Sale and(or) Use Coupons

Avoid Brand Loyalty

Use Simple Math

Pay Attention, Especially at Checkout

# Chapter 8

# Good Health Saves Money

Decrease spending and medical expenses through health promotion. The decrease in spending is attained primarily by eliminating, if applicable, the purchase of products and the habits that contribute to ill health and the multiple, negative, and costly consequences. The reduced expenses is primarily achieved by preventing high-priced medical interventions that would have been necessary.

Both Kathy and I do not use any tobacco products, do not drink any alcohol, and do not use illegal drugs; never have. As you will see, I have strong opinions on the use of cigarettes, alcohol, and illegal drugs.

Personal philosophy: I've been asked why I never smoked, drank, or used drugs, including to try or "experiment" with them in high school or college. My main reason was and is still: I do not see the need for cigarettes, alcohol, or illegal drugs. What is the need, reason, or excuse for drinking alcohol, either every day or on weekends? To feel happy, get drunk, or forget about life's problems? Does that make sense? Same with marijuana, cocaine, and heroin. And I never thought smelling like an ashtray made someone an adult or "cool."

**Spending** (I hope this topic does not apply to you.)

I do not spend any money on cigarettes or any other form of tobacco, alcohol from a store, bar, or restaurant, or illicit drugs. The direct lack of spending, just on not buying this stuff, is a tremendous cost avoidance. The cost savings on indirect spending is also huge.

Tobacco

The nicotine and cigarette habit/addiction drains a lot of money. A person spends about twenty dollars for one carton of cigarettes in Massachusetts. The state taxes on cigarettes usually dictates just how much one has to spend on the leading cause of avoidable morbidity and mortality in this country.

At two packs a day, smokers inhale approximately 14,600 cigarettes (or 73 cartons of cigarettes) in a year, for which the smokers spend about $1,460! That's $1,460 just in direct spending, the cost of the cancer-causing product.

Cigars, pipes, and chewing tobacco may not cost as much as cigarettes, but whatever they cost, cutting them out decreases spending.

Tobacco addiction results in many forms of indirect spending. In attempting to remove the film, coating and stench, you spend money on increased cleaning of many things: you, your hair, your clothes, the drapes and curtains, the light fixtures, the wallpaper or paint or both, the carpeting, the upholstery, the windows in your house and car, and the mirrors. Also buying cans of deodorizing spray for the air.

Alcohol

Millions of people spend hundreds of dollars each year on a mind-altering drug—alcohol. How much do you spend on drinking?

Whether fermented (beer and wine) or distilled (whiskey, gin, others), alcohol use and abuse (acknowledged or not) results in significant direct spending in different settings. Some people spend money in liquor stores and some supermarkets on alcohol for drinking at home and other places. Some people go to bars, taverns, or pubs and spend money specifically to drink alcohol. Some people spend extra money to drink alcohol at a restaurant where they already spend money for food, service, and atmosphere. And some people do all of the above.

My primary concern relates to people who spend money, in whatever setting, just for the sake of drinking alcohol, a few to several times a day, every day. It doesn't matter what form of the liquid drug one consumes. I can't think of any good, logical reason to drink a drug that can alter the mind and have other severe adverse health effects. Therefore, without true justification, there can only be rationalizations and excuses to spend hard-earned money on and drink alcohol.

My test for people who drink routinely: Try going for one week without drinking any alcohol. If you can't, you know that you have a problem, a big problem. If you go a week without drinking—fabulous. Please try two weeks. Then three weeks. After a month, ask yourself, "What did I miss?" If you do as well—or better—without the alcohol; what do you need the alcohol for? You learned that the drug was not only unnecessary, but detracted from enjoying nice things. That is the most valuable lesson, in addition to how much money you save.

Caution: If stop drinking and experience shaking of the hands, palpitations, rapid heartbeat, rapid breathing, nightmares, nausea, vomiting; especially with hallucinations, do two things. First, immediately seek medical attention, you are probably experiencing alcohol withdrawal. Second, recognize and admit you are an alcoholic, and get treatment.

If you believe you are at risk for alcohol withdrawal, check with your clinician for the safest approach to stop drinking, before trying to go without alcohol.

Illicit Drugs

From the previous two topics, I'm sure you know my opinion and recommendations about the use of illegal drugs and abuse of legal controlled substances (e.g., morphine, Percocet, Xanax, and Valium). What phony excuses do people have for doing drugs? They have too many problems or they are helpless and hopeless? Does heroin "help" a person? Why spend hundreds or thousands on drugs that abuse their bodies? Treatment is an investment in one's personal and financial health and well-being.

If applicable, please make treatment your first priority. Drug abuse is bigger than the mortgage war. Health first. Anyway, you will not win the mortgage war with your wages going in your nose, respiratory tract, or venous system. Enough said.

**Expenses**

Reduce medical expenses by decreasing, as much as you can, the need for expensive procedures and medications. Health promotion and preventative medicine reduces direct and indirect medical expenses.

Eliminate Bad Behaviors

Eliminate behaviors and activities that cause or contribute to diseases and ill health, especially tobacco, alcohol, and drug abuse.

You spend money buying cigarettes and then have the medical expenses as a consequence of smoking. Stop the smoking and decrease, at least, or eliminate the resultant medical expenses. And eliminate increased premiums on life insurance; for example, "tobacco rates" are twenty percent higher than "non-tobacco rates" at one company.

Alcohol has adverse effects on the brain, liver, gastrointestinal tract, and other organs, systems, and diseases of millions of Americans. Medical complications and expenses that result directly from alcohol include cirrhosis of the liver, fatty liver, gastritis, esophagitis, pancreatitis, and cancer (for alcoholics the risk is ten times greater than the general population). (*Harrison's Principles of Internal Medicine*, 13th ed. [McGraw Hill, 1994]) Please do not delude yourself into believing that alcohol is—all risks considered—beneficial. The possible cardiovascular benefit of a maximum of one to two drinks per day must be weighed against the multiple negative effects mentioned above, below (accidents and others), and other cardiovascular complications. Cardiovascular disease, including hypertension (high blood pressure), arrhythmias (abnormal heartbeats), and stroke, is the leading cause of death among alcoholics.

Abuse of illegal drugs, controlled substances, and the legal drug alcohol contribute to accidents while driving, at home (e.g., falls and fires), on the job (e.g., operating machinery), and boating (e.g., drowning and collisions), and contribute to violence. The accidents and violence caused by alcohol and drug abuse result in injuries, with medical expenses for the drinker or abuser, innocent people, or both. And fatalities. In addition, the risk of acquiring the human immunodeficiency virus (HIV) and AIDS is increased, principally from unprotected sex while drunk and intravenous drug abuse. Eliminate alcohol and eliminate a major factor in expensive and tragic events.

Eliminate tobacco, alcohol, and illicit drug use, which cause illness and injury, and you eliminate, or at least reduce, the need for medical care and medical expenses.

## If Obese, Lose Weight

Obesity is best defined as any degree of excess adipose tissue (fat) that imparts a health risk (*Harrison's Principles of Internal Medicine*, 13th ed. [McGraw Hill, 1994]). Forget looks and self-esteem; I'm talking major health risk.

Even mild obesity increases the risk for premature death, diabetes, high blood pressure (hypertension), narrowing of the arteries with plaque (atherosclerosis), gallbladder disease, and certain types of cancer. For example, type II, non-insulin dependent diabetes represents about ninety percent of the patients with diabetes in the United States. And eighty percent to ninety percent of patients with type 2 diabetes are obese. Obesity significantly contributes to the development of non-insulin dependent diabetes. Weight loss is an important treatment for these patients. There's an increased risk of blood clots, stroke, osteoarthritis (especially of the hips), sciatica, and varicose veins in obese individuals. (*Harrison's Principles of Internal Medicine*, 13th ed. [McGraw Hill, 1994])

Weight loss is essential for improved health and decreased medical expenses (avoiding diagnostic and surgical procedures, and medications). Get medical help to safely lose weight and minimize the risk of gaining back the excess pounds. Accomplish weight loss through diet and decreased caloric intake, behavior modification, and exercise. You feel better, breath easier, and enjoy many more activities with less weight. All positive reinforcement for your efforts.

Preventative Measures

Take preventative measures to promote your health and reduce medical expenses.

Wear your seat belt every time you are in an automobile, as the driver or a passenger, for short or long trips.

Be a responsible patient and participate in your health care, including any decision related to diagnosis and treatment. Get a physical examination annually, or as often as necessary. Do breast or testicular self exams. If on prescription or over-the-counter (OTC) medications, take as prescribed. Make sure each clinician responsible for your care knows all the medications, prescription and OTC, you take. Report any side or adverse effects to your clinician. Based on your condition, exercise regularly, both aerobic and strength. Avoid excessive sun exposure, especially between 10:00 A.M. and 3:00 P.M. Use sun block of SPF 15 or more (I use 30) that protects against both UVA and UVB rays. Also, please see Spending above.

Health promotion these days, unfortunately, includes avoiding assault and crimes. Better safe than sorry has never been a more appropriate expression, especially for women. Use common sense, do not take chances, and always think safety first. Of course, be reasonable. I wouldn't cross the street if I was walking and an elderly lady in a wheelchair came towards me. But if you feel uneasy when approached by someone, cross the street. When shopping, park your car as close to the store's exit as possible. And under a light when near or after dark. At home, never open the door to anyone you do not expect or do not know.

There are many more important steps to prevent crimes against you, wherever you are. Think first: What's the worst that can happen? Then do the safest thing.

Avoid accidents, please. Use common sense, do not take chances. Again, always think safety first. Don't get on a ladder until it's secure and steady. Wear eye protection in the workshop and anywhere else when using a hammer, circular saw, chain saw, and other tools. That way you are much more likely to be able to see the hammer the next time you need it. Do not use firecrackers or other fireworks. Don't stand on a chair that has castors, unless you enjoy short flights and limping. Avoid lifting heavy objects alone; get help. Avoid lifting any object from an awkward position; always face the object, have it as close to you as possible, and do not reach over at arms' length to lift. Use caution with a wet floor. Of course, there are many more examples.

Learn from other people's accidents and mistakes. No need for you to prove that a firecracker can blow your fingers or hand off; that has been well established. I learned a couple of things about accidents when I tried to make apple crisp quickly at the age of twelve. I cut up the apples, put them in a pyrex dish, covered the apples with cinnamon sugar, and heated the dish on the stove. The dish exploded like a hand grenade. Fortunately, I was in the pantry at the time of the blast and wasn't hurt. I learned that a pyrex dish does not heat well over a direct flame. And I learned that haste not only makes waste; haste can be dangerous.

In contrast to the ad slogan "just do it"—please stop and think before doing it. What's the worst thing that can happen? What are the consequences of the worst thing happening?

It may take a little longer to do something the smartest way, rather than the quickest way. You can rush, use a ladder a dozen times without stabilizing it, and not fall off. However, if you fall off a ladder once, you may have a temporary or permanent disability. You could miss work and lose income. It may be more difficult or costly to get medical insurance in the future. And everyone— individuals, businesses, and the government—all pay higher insurance premiums because of medical care for accidents. The cost of higher insurance rates for businesses and government are passed along in higher prices for their goods and services, and taxes, respectively. So directly and indirectly, we all pay for accidents.

Is the benefit of doing something quickly, such using a ladder without stabilizing it, greater than the risk and consequences of an accident? Understandably, it's sometimes difficult to recognize the advantage of something that doesn't happen. Some people do not appreciate the benefits of stopping, thinking, and avoiding an accident until they have one. From then on, the person always takes the time to secure a ladder; if the individual can still walk.

Avoid accidental poisoning, especially with children. Many poisons are commonly in the house: cleaners, stains and paints, alcohol, prescription and OTC medications, and certain plants. Never leave hazardous substances out, even for just a few minutes. Keep cleaners and painting materials in a locked cabinet. Keep all medications, including aspirin and cough and cold preparations, out of the reach of children. And don't say their medicine is candy. Certain pediatric medicine almost tastes too good and kids think the medication is a treat. Some adults, even without arthritis or poor vision, have trouble getting the childproof cap off, but do not leave it off for convenience. Have the Poison Control Center telephone number handy. But prevention is most important.

## Summary

How much are tobacco products, alcohol, and drug abuse costing you, directly in spending and indirectly in medical expenses? Nothing, I hope. If you do use tobacco, alcohol, or drugs illegally, please stop. Get help, if necessary. I know, it's easy for me to say. But you'll be glad you did. For your health reasons first and financial reasons second.

Take preventative measures for your health, including using common sense and avoiding accidents.

You want to be able to enjoy the benefits of achieving the ultimate goal in good health.

# Chapter 9

# Decrease Expenses Around the House

You use numerous tactics to decrease expenses and save a lot of money around the house. These expenses include electricity, gas or oil, water, and telephone bills. Many tactics reduce expenses on a daily, every other day or weekly basis; therefore, the savings are tremendous over a long period of time.

Although some ways to save money are somewhat inconvenient or a little more time-consuming, the total savings are substantial and help pay off the mortgage. In addition, the around-the-house tactics are all part of your mindset for saving money. Increasing organization and efficiency helps offset time-consuming measures.

Other worthwhile tactics involve changing habits (e.g., set thermostats at different temperatures) or an investment (e.g., attic insulation).

Tactics vary based on your location, the seasons, and the climate. Some steps may appear obvious and you wonder why you didn't think of them. A few practices may appear impractical, but please give them a try. And you may have some of your own money-saving methods.

One easy step is to read the owner's manual for appliances. The manuals should have specific recommendations for efficient use and energy savings.

I discuss the tactics on a room or activity basis. Here we go, around the house.

## Kitchen

Dishwasher

The dishwasher expense is the energy for the hot water heater, the water itself, dishwasher detergent, electricity, and repairs. The dishwasher savings comes from planning and organization, using the short washing cycle, and open air drying.

Never run the dishwasher unless it's full. First use the sink, hand dishwashing liquid soap, and limited water to soak and clean off the dishes. Leave a soap film on the dishes and don't rinse before loading. This saves water, makes dishwasher cleaning easier, and decreases the debris in the machine.

Plan ahead when you load the dishwasher. Arrange the dishes in a way that maximizes the amount you fit in the dishwasher and allows efficient return of the dishes to the cabinet. If you stack smaller plates on top of larger plates in the cabinet, line up the larger and smaller plates in the dishwasher. Planning ahead saves time unloading. Save footsteps; have the dish cabinet over and silverware drawer next to the dishwasher.

Use the short, light wash or quick cycle (vs. the longer, normal cycle) every time. The light cycle does a great job, uses less electricity and hot water, uses only half of the detergent (one dispenser vs. two), and takes less time than the normal cycle. Less time means reduced wear and tear on the machine, fewer costly repairs, and less noise.

In general, medium water requires less detergent than hard water, and soft water requires the least amount of detergent. Check with your water department for hardness information and your dishwasher manual for specific instructions on filling the detergent dispenser. Using too much detergent increases costs unnecessarily and may harm the dishes. The powder frequently cakes; so I use the liquid dishwasher detergent.

When the wash and rinse cycles are complete and the dry cycle is about to begin, shut off the dishwasher (with the wall switch, dial, or lever) and open the door minimally. Allow the steam to escape slowly. After about five minutes, open the dishwasher completely, remove any water that may have collected in containers or the bottoms of cups, place the silverware basket in the counter drainer (for better air drying), pull out the dishes and the glasses racks, and allow the dishes to open air dry. This technique works great overnight or the dishes dry in about an hour. Just in case you forget to open air dry, select the dishwasher's energy saving, air, or fan dry cycle.

Sink

Install an inexpensive, aerator water-saving device in the spout. The best way to conserve water and save money on hot water is to squirt a sufficient amount of hand dishwashing liquid detergent on the dishes, glasses, silverware, and pots and pans, run enough water to create suds and wet all the items, and shut off the water. Let the items with dried on or crusty food soak a little, then use the sponge, soap pad, or Brillo.

Put the dishes, glasses, and silverware in the dishwasher with a soap film. Rinse off the pots and pans together (and dishes, etc., if you don't have a dishwasher) so that some rinse water flows off one item onto and over another, and place the rinsed pots and pans in the drainer to air dry.

Refrigerator

The refrigerator is plugged in all the time; so energy efficiency is important when buying a refrigerator. Buy one large enough for storage, especially freezing, of food bought on sale in quantity.

Minimize the use, expense, and possible waste of electricity. Select the most appropriate temperature setting, not too cold. Whenever possible, use the energy-saving feature. Locate the refrigerator away from a heat source and make sure there's adequate space behind, over, and on the sides for proper ventilation. Regularly vacuum the grills in front and behind.

Know what you want before opening the refrigerator or freezer, especially in the summer. The refrigerator is an inefficient air conditioner. Keep the contents of the refrigerator and freezer organized, including labeling items that you froze (with the name and date [rotate stock]); so you can find things fast. Do not block the freezer air vents. Choose the correct temperature/moisture settings for the meat, vegetable, and fruit compartments.

Live without an automatic ice dispenser and water dispenser. They are expensive options (original cost plus the plumber), even if they do save opening the freezer door.

## Garbage and Trash

Please recycle whenever possible. It's a little inconvenient, but relatively easy. Thank you for recycling.

Small tangent alert: If you don't know your community's recycling policy, please check with the town or city hall to see what can be recycled and how to go about it (e.g., curbside pickup or bring material to a recycling center). It's possible to recycle many things: aluminum cans, foil, trays, and objects, steel ("tin") cans and objects, opaque containers (e.g., milk jugs), clear and colored plastic, clear and colored glass, newspapers, cardboard, oil (please do not put any oil down storm drains), and batteries (car and home). The metal cans usually have the type of metal in the recycling symbol (the arrow triangle) on the label. The plastic containers have the recycling code (e.g., HDPE 2 or PETE 1) with the number in the arrow symbol, on the bottom. If you have a deposit on beverage containers, return them to the store for the deposit refund. The store will recycle the bottles.

Recycling is extremely important for the environment, well worth the effort, and feels good. Please encourage your friends and neighbors to recycle. Organize recycling projects, such as with the Cub Scouts. Increased recycling will have more benefits: increased efficiency and economics for reprocessing materials, decreased taxes for waste disposal, and decreased costs of product packaging. Some people use some or most of their garbage for composting, but I haven't tried that yet.

Don't buy kitchen garbage bags or trash bags. Use plastic grocery bags for garbage and paper grocery bags for trash. The paper bags fit nicely under the sink or in a plastic kitchen trash receptacle. Keep your bag needs in mind at the supermarket when asked about paper or plastic.

When buying thirty gallon trash bags for curbside or dump disposal, sacrifice the convenience and increased expense of the colorful tie handles for the savings of a basic bag. The trash doesn't know the difference.

Do not use the garbage disposal routinely; decrease water use, wear and tear, repair bills, and accidents (rings, silverware, and worse).

Microwave Oven

If you do not have a microwave oven, please buy one. A good microwave is a need and an investment, not just a want and a convenience. A microwave dramatically increases efficiency, saves a lot of time, and is great for defrosting, preparing or cooking, and reheating many foods.

A high quality microwave with preprogrammed cooking is more expensive, but it's an excellent value. A microwave saves many hundreds of dollars over dining out regularly. I bought a Sharp Carousel II microwave with SensorCook (on sale) in 1985 and it's still fabulous. An increased use of electricity by a microwave, is offset by a decreased use of gas or electricity by a stove and conventional oven (and air conditioning in the summer to compensate for the oven).

Prepare fresh or frozen vegetables (much better than canned), baked potatoes, bacon, meat loaf, and much more in minutes. Need to reheat something during dinner? Thirty seconds and the food is hot again. Cleanup is easier and faster because you usually prepare the food on the plates you use at the table and there are fewer pots and pans to clean. This saves water, detergent, hot water heater expenses, and time. Place the microwave near the kitchen table, dishes, preparation area, and refrigerator; efficient and convenient.

**Laundry**

Reduce expenses, save natural resources, and still have clean clothes, towels, and linens. Except for items that must be dry-cleaned, wash and dry everything at home.

Washing Machine

For most laundry items, the washing machine's shortest (usually delicate) cycle works very well, and saves water, electricity, and wear and tear on the machine.  I use the short cycle for everything except bed linen (use longer, permanent press cycle) and men's cotton undershirts, underwear, and socks (cotton cycle). Even large, cotton bath towels, used three or four times, get the shortest cycle and do great. After all, you're already clean when using the towels.

Use the cold wash and cold rinse for all laundry. I realize this approach is contrary to the recommendations of manufacturers of the clothing, linen, towels, and  laundry detergents. However, the cold/cold selection works fine, eliminates hot water costs, and reduces shrinkage.

Sort laundry properly, balance the laundry around the agitator, and do full loads. Select the lowest, appropriate water level; enough water to cover the laundry and have adequate agitation and rinsing. Measure the laundry detergent, don't just pour it in. I use the liquid because the powder cakes. Please remember, although phosphorous in the detergent softens the water, phosphorous can contribute to water pollution.

Important: When the washing machine is not in use, shut off the water to the machine. Do you have a lever that easily controls the hot and cold water to the washer? Use it.  If not, shut off the water at the faucet.  It is worth the effort. If left open/on, the water pressure builds up in the hoses, eventually they bulge, and ultimately, they burst. Pop. Costly water damage and messy cleanup. Inspect the full length of your hoses. If you see a bulge in one or both, replace both hoses.

Drying Racks

For drying, buy three or four drying racks (on sale) to dry most items, especially in good weather. The metal racks with the plastic covering on the dowels are best.  Metal racks last much longer than wooden ones.  The wooden racks can crack, the dowels can loosen and come out, and the dowels can discolor (mold?) when wet. A sweater rack is useful at times too. On warm sunny days, I dry almost everything outside on the racks.

Drying on the back deck saves electricity (or gas) and wear and tear on the dryer. The laundry gets fresh air and smells nice. The towels, clothes, and other laundry last longer; the lint collected in the dryer comes from something—the fabric. Also, I save energy and natural resources.

A laundry placement system that works well for me:  pajama and sweat suit tops, blouses and tee shirts do nicely hanging around the end; the pants lie flat on the three dowels going upward at an angle in the middle; always with adequate room for air circulation. You may have to turn the racks around and turn the towels over to face the sun, at times. The towels are stiffer than from the drier. Lay large bed linen over two racks to dry.  No big deal.

My deck is conveniently located next to the laundry room. No matter what the distance for you, it's worth the trip to the deck, patio, or sunny area.

Incidentally, a neighborhood covenant prohibits clotheslines (and farm animals, among other things), but not drying racks. But you could use a clothesline, as I did at my first house.  I'm not particularly concerned about what the neighbors think.  There is a fair amount of space between houses.  More important, drying laundry on the deck is a tactic that helped us own the deck, and the rest of the property, outright in two years.

During the winter, I dry as much laundry as possible on the racks indoors. Of course it takes longer, at least overnight. The towels and the bed linen are dried in the dryer.

Dryer

When using the dryer, save energy and money.  First, separate the wet items as you put them in the dryer.  This allows better air circulation and more efficient drying (vs. the laundry being clumped together).  Do not use a timed cycle. The drier may continue to run long after the clothes are dry.  Instead, use the lowest setting that works on the more dry/less dry option.  You may experiment a little to see if, for example, 2 on a 1 to 6 dial, is sufficient.  Extra drying time is needed occasionally; better than overkill every time. Always clean out the lint collector after each use to increase efficiency.

Again, wash and dry at home anything that can be washed and dried at home.  The only time I use a commercial laundry is for garments and a wool blanket that require dry-cleaning.

**Bathrooms**

To conserve water and money, install a water-saving, flow restrictor (aerator) in all bathroom sink faucets and shower heads.

While brushing your teeth, only use the water when needed. Don't let the water run continuously. As a test, close the drain while running the water and brushing your teeth. You will be amazed how quickly the water overflows. A water conservation ad said that if you had to drink all the water wasted while brushing your teeth, you would never get out of the bathroom.

There are similar savings when shaving with lather and a razor. Instead of running the water constantly, partially fill the sink once and rinse off the razor in the small pond.

Save water while washing your face and hands; lather with the water off and rinse with the water flow reduced.

A shower uses more water than a bath.  If you take showers, be ready to go in when the water is hot and don't stand there any longer than necessary.

If you do not have water-conserving toilets, install a water-saving dam in each toilet. A newer, water-conserving toilet uses approximately 1.5 gallons of water per flush. A toilet about three years to twenty years old uses approximately 3.5 gallons of water per flush.  A toilet older than twenty years uses about 5 to 6 gallons per flush.

Speaking of flushes, for other than a newer toilet, do you truly need to flush the toilet after urinating once?  Not really. You can use the toilet for urine three or four times over a few hours without flushing and without adverse effects.  (Leaving it overnight is another story.)  This practice saves water, 3.5 to 6 gallons per flush, many times a day, every day for years, and wear and tear on the toilet. How much fresh water could be saved nationally?

Considering the number of times you brush your teeth, shave, wash your face and hands, shower and urinate in a year, the water and dollar savings are tremendous.

## Hot Water Heater

Adjust the hot water heater thermostat to the minimum appropriate temperature; decrease gas or electricity expenses, and decrease the risk of accidental scalding, especially with children. Check the dishwasher owner's manual for the recommended hot water temperature.

## Heating

The reduced expenses comes from minimizing the use of gas, oil, or electricity for heating, increasing heating efficiency, and reducing heat loss (from a living space to a non-living space [attic/basement] and from the inside to the outside of the house).

Minimize Heating

Evaluate the temperatures you maintain in the house and consider each zone individually. I have the thermostat set at sixty-five degrees for the room(s) I am in, and only while I am there (including the bedroom overnight). When I'm not in a room, day or night, the thermostat is set at sixty degrees.

I wear a robe on arising and a sweat suit (under a down parka [just kidding]) during the day, and use a couple of comforters during the night. This works well. I am comfortable wherever I am and it's not too chilly for the plants and, most importantly, the wonderful kitty cat.

Increase Heating Efficiency

For maximal efficiency, vacuum the heating registers on a regular basis during the winter. Maintain adequate space around the registers for proper distribution of heat.

As the seasons change and the windows are open during the day and the heat is on at night, remember to either switch off the heat or turn the thermostat down to the lowest setting when you open the windows.

Insulate the heating ducts or pipes in the basement to maximize the heat delivered throughout the house and minimize heating the basement.

Reduce Heat Loss

Insulate the attic very well. In addition to the insulation between the joists, put at least another twelve inches of fiberglass insulation (or the equivalent) on top of the joists.  I used the rolls of unfaced (no paper) insulation, unrolled perpendicular to the joists. The fiberglass should be as fluffy as possible.  Matting it down or bunching it up decreases the insulation effect. Do not put insulation where the roof meets the side of the house; allow adequate space for ventilation to avoid water condensation. Insulation between the roof rafters is unnecessary, unless you regularly spend time in the attic or use it as a living space.

Caution: Wear work gloves, full eye protection (goggles), a mask over the mouth and nose, a long sleeve shirt, and long pants when handling fiberglass insulation.

Make sure the attic is thoroughly ventilated, with a roof vent (along the peak) or a gable louver vent at both ends/peaks of the attic.  A few soffit vents alone are essentially ineffective.

Insulate between the joists in the ceiling of the basement.

Evaluate heat loss from windows and doors. How much of a draft is there around the edges?  An occasional little draft is permissible and allows fresh air into the house. Weather stripping is necessary to prevent large heat loss.

Heat is even lost through interior electrical outlets on outside walls (not walls separating rooms). If you feel cold air at the socket, there is heat loss. Flat plastic plugs in unused sockets are useful.

Keep the shades down, especially for large windows and on cloudy days.  On sunny days, the sunlight may help warm a room a little and lift your spirits during the winter.

Close the fireplace flue when you are not enjoying a fire. The flue must be open when using the fireplace. A glassdoor firescreen reduces the heat lost from the house up the chimney and decreases the risk of burning embers escaping into the house.

If you have any type of air conditioning, close all vents.

Your electric or gas utility, or local environmental protection group may do a heat loss and energy efficiency analysis and give specific recommendations for a small fee or free. They may also have heat-saving devices at a discount price.

Please be aware a house may be too "tight" and prevent enough fresh air from entering the home. This is a problem for some people.

## Cooling

On hot and humid summer days and nights I am delighted I have central air conditioning (AC). The AC significantly increases the quality of life. The initial expense for installation (in my new house before I moved in) and the cost of electricity each summer are needs. Several tactics increase AC efficiency, minimize the electricity expense, and save money.

Central Air Conditioning

In installation and maintenance, the air conditioning unit(s) should be out of the direct sun and have plenty of space around them for air circulation. Clean the air intake vents in your home and regularly change the filter. The frequency depends on the amount of use and dust in the air. The large tubing that carries the cool air should be well insulated and have a tight connection to the AC vents for each room. Regularly vacuum the AC vents in the rooms and keep them wide open.

Most important, set the thermostat at the highest temperature that's comfortable. I anticipate the need for AC based on weather forecasts of increased temperature or increased humidity or both; I turn on the AC the evening before. It's easier for the system to work, especially getting started, without Mr. Sunshine heating up everything. The AC provides relief by removing heat and humidity from the air. Therefore, set the thermostat based on your comfort from reduced humidity, not just air temperature.

Of course, all doors to the outside and windows must be closed. In addition, draw the window shades down all the way, particularly on the sunny sides. Minimize or eliminate the use of the conventional oven. I really appreciate the outdoor grill and microwave oven. The attic insulation that helps keep the house warm in the winter also helps the AC keep the house cool and comfortable in the summer. Shade from large trees reduce the effects of summer sun on the house.

Room or Built-In Air Conditioning

Reduce expenses from room or built-in air conditioners using several tactics mentioned above. Turn on the AC in the evening. Close the door to the room or have the area closed off, based on the size and effectiveness of the unit. How large a space is the unit capable of cooling? If the space is too large for the unit, the efficiency is decreased, the electricity use is increased, and the unit will need repairs sooner. Close the shades during the day, especially on the sunny sides. If possible, avoid placing the room or built-in unit in full sun; partial shade is preferable and full shade is splendid. Use weather stripping or similar devices to seal the unit and avoid losing the benefit of the AC through cracks. Cover the unit and close the vent for the winter, if applicable.

Air conditioning is a necessary expense. Simple measures reduce the expense and save money.

**Telephone**

Based on your calling patterns, Do you have the most economical local and long distance telephone service? No basic rates. Check with your local telephone company and review all discount plans. The same for your long distance carrier and its competitors. Perhaps you changed jobs, or family or friends moved away from the area. Could an alternative plan decrease your telephone expenses?

If family or friends have local phone plans that don't cost them extra to call you, ask them to call you back or set up a signal system for them to call you (e.g., after you call them and let it ring once).

Know when you can save money and when making a call will cost you more. Long distance and local toll rates are usually classified as day, evening, and night/weekend, the most to least expensive, respectively. Make long distance calls anytime on Saturday or on Sunday before 5:00 P.M., at the lowest, night/weekend rate. At least wait until after 5:00 P.M. during the week for the lower, evening rate.

My best local service plan has a base charge for up to 120 minutes per month within a certain calling area. Any time over the two hours costs $0.052 per minute. Until recently, the exception was between 9:00 A.M. and noon, when every call outside the immediate area was a toll call at a much more expensive charge per minute. Unless you had an 800 or local number, you didn't get any calls from me between nine and noon.

Do you really need and actually use each of the extra services (e.g., automatic redial by the phone company) you pay for month after month? Are these extra services just conveniences that increase your phone bill?

Making telephone calls should not be an impulse behavior. Could you delay the call a few minutes, a couple of hours, or wait until the weekend to save money? Does the business you're calling have a toll-free number? You can check with 800 information at 1-800-555-1212. Is there a charge for use or excessive use of local information? The telephone company provides phone books for your area and other sections within your region at no charge. Use telephone books and note numbers you frequently call in your address book or on a note card for convenience.

Please do not call 900 numbers. You don't have to be a psychic to know these numbers are gimmicks. I have a feeling the 900 numbers run up your telephone expenses rapidly, usually at dollars per minute.

What is your telephone expense over a year? Three tactics reduce telephone expenses: you have the best local and best long distance discount calling plans, you have only necessary services, and most important, you think before making any telephone calls— no impulse calls.

## Clean Up and Organization

If you pay someone to clean the house, this is classified as a convenience that increases your spending of discretionary funds; money that should be going to pay off your mortgage. A housekeeper is not a necessity and not an expense (like electricity). Decrease your spending; do the housecleaning yourselves. I realize that if you are used to a housekeeper doing your work, doing it yourself may be easier written than done.

Equitable division of household missions and good organization are the keys to a clean and happy home. You have the fun of dividing or sharing the tasks around the house, based on your individual situation. Improve household organization.

Increase the space for you and the things you need—get rid of junk. Clean out the house by asking yourself three questions: Is the item used regularly, periodically/seasonally, or at least annually? Is the item needed for an emergency or saved for your records? And is the item a keepsake, memorabilia, or valuable? If the answer for each question is no, out it goes; donation, recycle, or trash.

The old saying applies, there should be a place for everything and everything should be in its place. Try to handle things only once; put items in their appropriate place (e.g., wastebasket, desk, closet, filing cabinet, recycling area) when you first touch them. Keep things under control. Be neat and avoid aggravation; clean up little messes before the little messes accumulate into big, frustrating messes. Establish "no junk" zones; places where no one dumps stuff, such as the kitchen island. Have the stereo or television on to provide a pleasant atmosphere for cleanup and other household activities.

The same principles apply for tasks around the outside the house. Do not pay anyone to take care of your lawn. Fertilize, water, mow, and trim the lawn yourself. Create and maintain flower beds and gardens yourself. Have the appropriate amount of a nice mulch delivered and apply it yourself. When it snows, clear the driveway and walk yourself. You probably have noticed a theme: Do it yourself. You save hundreds of dollars and have a sense of satisfaction and accomplishment.

You need to know your limits. Tree work can be difficult and dangerous. You may be able to cut down and cut up small trees. But large trees can hurt you or your house. You may need a professional who knows what he is doing and is insured (be sure he is insured). When the snow is too deep or too heavy, have the driveway plowed. Your back, heart, and health are the first priority. Painting or staining your house may or may not be something you can do yourself. Fear of heights is a major drawback. And you don't want to make a mess of your most expensive purchase. But you can stain your deck. So get some fresh air and exercise, as well as the satisfaction of doing outside tasks yourself.

Keep focused on your mortgage goal and have a do-it-yourself mindset. They pay off sooner than later.

### Summary

Living in a house has many costs, including electricity, heating, cooling, and telephone. These and other expenses add up to thousands of dollars over each year. The consistent use of the many tactics to decrease expenses around the inside and outside of your home reinforces the mortgage priority and money-saving mindset and allows you to put the thousands of dollars saved to win the mortgage war.

# Part IV

# The Winning Tactics

## Real Estate
## and Banking

Chapter 10

# Get the Most Money
# Selling Your House

You want to get the most money for your house as reasonably possible and (usually) sell the house as soon as possible.

Whether you try For Sale By Owner or use a real estate agent, before the first prospective buyer pulls up to the curb, use the most important tactics in selling your house: price it right and make the perfect presentation and impression (PPI).

Negotiating the selling price is also important, but without the right offering price and PPI, you won't get an offer to negotiate.

**For Sale By Owner or Real Estate Agent**

About the only advantage of selling your house yourself is saving the sales commission, usually about six percent of the selling price. You can either pocket the savings or use the savings to discount the offering and selling price, making the house more attractive to buyers.

There are many reasons why real estate agents sell many more houses than homeowners. These reasons include: agents know what they're doing, they sell houses for a living (How many houses have you sold?); agents use multiple listing services, making your house available to a huge market; agents screen and "qualify" (assess and confirm ability to get a mortgage) buyers before they show your house, minimizing visits from people who were just taking a ride on a Sunday afternoon and saw your For Sale sign; agents use a lockbox (house key accessible in a locked box near the front door) and can show your house when you are at work or away; and agents help you with candid (don't be insulted) information on presenting and pricing your home.

How do you find a good agent? First, do you know a real estate agent as a friend or from a previous transaction? If not, do your homework. Ask friends and neighbors who have sold and bought houses. Look around town. Seeing several For Sale signs by a realtor is favorable (provided the signs are not on the lawn for a long time). Visit and talk with a few agents. Ask how they would market your house. Advertising in local papers and larger Sunday newspapers. Multiple listing service or services. National service for people relocating to your area. Open houses. Do they know your neighborhood, the local school, and school system? Ask for and check references. What is your impression of the realty office and the agent? Would you buy a house from that office and agent?

A good agent offers useful information on pricing and selling your home, markets aggressively, and keeps you informed. The right real estate agent makes a big difference selling your home.

**The Right Price**

Like Goldie Locks, you need the offering price to be just right. Serious buyers usually only consider houses they can afford. If your price is too high, some buyers who really can afford the house, never see it. And if they see your high-priced house, the competition looks good. If your price is too low, some buyers may think something is wrong with the property or think it's not good enough to meet their needs—you undervalue the property. Even though the house is a bargain, some buyers never see it. Also, when you do sell, you give the house away and have less money for a down payment on your next house. You need the right offering price.

Also consider how much money you need from the sale of the house (after the sales commission) and how fast you need to sell the house, usually the sooner the better.

Big Deal: When you win, or preferably since you won, the mortgage war—you have 100 percent equity—every dime of the selling price (minus the sales commission) can go to the down payment for the next house.

## Determining Property Value

Determine the value of your property—and the right price—objectively. The real estate agent provides up-to-date (past six months to current) information on the real estate market in your area and neighborhood: the asking prices, selling prices, and length of time on the market. The same information that potential buyers should be considering when looking at your house and other houses. The real estate market is subject to change and a price adjustment may be necessary.

Mortgage interest rates, of course, influence the real estate market. In general, when interest rates are low, more people can afford to buy, demand for houses goes up, and prices increases; a seller's market. When interest rates are high, fewer people can afford to buy, demand for houses goes down, and prices decrease; a buyer's market.

Based on the above information, first determine the right price range for your property. Higher-valued properties have a wider price range in actual dollars, but about the same percentage range, as lower-valued houses. Should you price the house in the high end, middle, or low end of the range? Consider your selling points.

## The Selling Points

Objectively, what specific selling points does your house offer and not offer. First, as usual, is location. Nice, quiet neighborhood, with easy access to commuting routes, increases the value. Unkept, noisy neighborhood, with railroad tracks behind the house, decreases the value.

You may take certain features for granted; walk around the house as if you're a buyer. What gets your attention? Big deck. Four good-sized bedrooms. Whirlpool bath. Level lot with a great view of the lake. All great selling points. Emphasize features that distinguish your house from others in the neighborhood.

## Remodeling

Even if your house is old (so are the other houses in the neighbor-hood), if you remodeled within two or three years—in the right ar-eas—you increase the value of your house. Consider two types of remodeling: minor and major.

## Minor remodeling

Minor remodeling is primarily maintenance and repairs, the basics. Make sure everything works and, at least, looks good, if not great. Every window and door opens and closes properly, doorknobs and hand rails are fastened properly, toilets and faucets function prop-erly, everything. Unless you market the house as a low-priced, fix-it-upper: replace worn carpeting (install neutral color) or clean dirty carpeting, fix (really, not just cover-up) or replace an old roof, sand and finish hardwood floors, upgrade plumbing. It's difficult for the buyer to focus on the whirlpool bath with the shower constantly dripping.

## Major remodeling

Major remodeling of your kitchen and bathrooms makes you feel good and is a good investment. You get back in the selling price nearly all the money you spend to remodel the kitchen and bath-rooms, as long as you don't recreate the Taj Mahal. Do not over-spend. First, overpriced remodeling will not blend with the rest of the house, making the rest of the house look old and in need of up-dating. Second, you just do not get your money back in the sale. In the kitchen and bathrooms, remember form and function first.

In the kitchen, everybody loves spacious counters and cabinets, well-lit cooking and dining areas, and updated appliances. After the bathroom essentials, a whirlpool bath is an attractive addition. Emotionally, a whirlpool was one of the features we looked for in buying our house. Practically, we rarely use the whirlpool. Still, it's a good selling point, when the rest of the bathroom looks good too. A room addition, such as a a family room or sunroom, in the style of the home, usually has a good return on investment.

Some remodeling does not pay off at sale, such as converting a garage to a room, finishing a basement, or adding a pool. In fact, because of the fear of drowning, a pool may deter buyers with small children.

Painting

Painting may be the least expensive, and most important, step in remodeling (assuming you have paint, not wallpaper . . . oops, paper wallcovering). Stains and marks on walls make a bad impression on buyers. What about paint colors? Purple is your favorite color. How many buyers like purple, especially for the master bedroom wall? Bold colors distract buyers. Neutral colors may not excite people, but off-white and beige are comfortable colors and better for selling the house. When the potential buyers drive away, you want them talking about the spacious kitchen or big deck, not the purple bedroom. A recent coat or two of paint is a selling point and important for presentation.

Pay attention to the appearance of the outside too. If the house, trim, front door, picket fence, hand rails, trellis, mailbox, mailbox post or anything else needs to be painted or stained, do it; you get your money back and sell the house faster. Again, neutral colors. Wash dirty aluminum or vinyl siding, and the front door. Sweep the driveway and apply new sealer (mostly for appearance).

The selling points, in addition to the real estate market, the amount of money you need from the sale, and how quickly you need to sell, determine the right offering price. Now it's time to market the house.

**Perfect Presentation and Impression**

Presentation starts before the buyers' car engine stops. You need to make a great impression from the moment the buyers first see your property until they start their car to head back home. When you create a great impression and feeling, the positive feelings continue long after the buyers leave your house.

You must have great "curb appeal": the first impression the buyers have when they drive up to your property. Buyers start to picture themselves living in the house. Painting or staining the house, trim, picket fence, and other things mentioned above is the first step to establish curb appeal. Repair broken steps, cracked walks, and loose gutters and downspouts. Put new mulch down, clean up leaves, get rid of weeds, plant flowers, and trim hedges and bushes. Make sure the grass looks good, nicely mowed and edged. Perfect.

Buyers want a nice neighborhood and expect to pay more for a house (i.e., your house) in a nice neighborhood. Ask neighbors to keep their property neat. Everyone wins: your house sells for more, increasing the neighbors' property values.

All your efforts outside—everything looks great and well maintained—pay off by creating critical curb appeal. It can even attract a potential buyer just driving by and seeing the For Sale sign and nice property.

As the buyers leave their car and approach the front door with the light fixtures cleaned, and the new, basic (not cute) welcome mat, favorable impressions continue to set the tone for walking through the house. Impressions become favorable feelings, especially when the inside meets the high expectations created by the outside.

Make the first thing the buyers see when they walk in comfortable and welcoming, not distracting. Although some personal items around the house makes it homey, it's better to be restrained and minimize photographs and mementos. You want buyers to think of themselves in their future home. Incidentally, a vacant house is usually more difficult to sell because it doesn't look or feel like a home.

Attention to detail and neatness count: for more dollars and quicker sale. You made repairs and did some remodeling, now maintain show condition every day. The little things mean a lot—of money. Think spacious and neat, clean and bright.

Make your house spacious and neat; get rid of all junk. Buyers look everywhere (attic, basements, closets [how much space?]). Get rid of junk everywhere. You can have a yard sale, donate the stuff, or dispose of it properly. Your house looks bigger, even the kitchen cabinets look roomier, with less clutter. Also, you have less to move to the new house. Straighten out books, newspapers, and magazines. Make the beds and put dirty laundry in hampers. Keep everything neat and orderly so you don't have a crisis if the phone rings and your agent apologizes, saying she needs to show the house in an hour.

Make your house clean and keep it clean every day (a tough task); the next appointment could make the sale. Even a fix-it-upper should be clean. Clean the windows, inside and out, and the mirrors. Polish the furniture. The kitchen and bathrooms must sparkle every day. Odors distract: no tobacco, pet, or other odors. Potpourri in the bathroom is good, but clean is better. You won't need air fresheners that try to cover odors. No dust, dirt, film, grease, or residue anywhere. No dishes or pans in the sink or stuff on the kitchen counters. Trash and garbage taken out, kept in a covered container. Do a walk through before a showing and before you leave the house in the morning to make sure everything is picked up and clean. With the lockbox, you never know when someone may see the house during the day.

Make the house bright. Leave the shades up and open the curtains, especially where the sun shines. Avoid blocking sunlight with furniture. When the sun starts to set, turn on lots of lights. A bright house enhances the mood.

Keep the house spacious and neat, clean and bright. It's an inexpensive way to increase the selling price. Do it as if thousands of dollars depend on it.

### Take a Ride or a Long Walk

When the house is shown by the agent, try to somewhere, anywhere, else. You want the buyers comfortable, taking their time, without the homeowner looking over their shoulders.

The agent is familiar with the property and can answer questions. The agent usually prepares a fact sheet about the listing. The potential buyers can take a fact sheet and refer to the sheet during the visit and take it home. If any questions come up the agent can't answer, get back to the potential buyers later.

If you have a pet(s), make arrangements to keep the pet in a part of the basement or a particular room during a showing, unless the pet is a goldfish. You may need to stay on the property with the pet during a showing or take the doggie for a walk.

## Negotiating the Selling Price

You did great presenting the house, now you have an offer from a buyer; time to negotiate. Your original offering price is right, based on the real estate market, the net amount of money you need from the sale (after the agent's commission), the time frame for selling, and the selling points of your house.

The three big questions: How does the buyers' offer compare with your offering price and the net amount of money you need from the sale? How long has the house been on the market? And who are the buyers?

If you won the mortgage war you know every last dime of the selling price (less the sales fee) is yours. You do not have to pay the principal balance, because there is no principal left. Therefore, you can be a little flexible in negotiating and determining the net amount of money you need from the sale.

Established in ancient times, the negotiating rule is: the seller's willingness to negotiate is directly proportional to the time the property has not sold. The longer your house has been on the market the more willing you are to negotiate. And the reverse is true.

It helps to learn about the buyers. Are they in a hurry? Do they reeeally love the house? Is this the first house they saw? Have they shopped around for a long time and finally found there dream house? The answers influence your negotiating tactics.

The final variable in negotiating is your gut feeling. You don't want to give your house away, but you don't want to keep yourself from moving to your new house either. Remember, if the house has been on the market for a while and this is your first and only offer, a bird in the hand is worth more than none (not two) in the bush.

## Purchase and Sale Agreement

When you and the buyers agree on the selling price, it's time to sign the purchase and sale agreement (P and S) and celebrate. You receive a signed P and S and a deposit or earnest money from the buyers. You and your agent give a receipt for the deposit. The deposit can and should, for the buyers' protection, be put in an escrow account.

Read the P and S before signing, it's a legal contract. The agreement is usually a standard document, but have your lawyer review the P and S if you are uncomfortable signing it.

Some contingencies may be included in the P and S, such as a professional home inspection. You should not be worried about the home inspection for two reasons. One, you already checked the house thoroughly and did all the necessary repairs and maintenance; there should be no surprises. Two, you disclosed in advance any and all defects in the house, the buyers were aware of the defects and the plans (defects will be repaired or selling price adjusted). Make sure the defects are noted in writing. You don't want the buyer suing you later, saying they were not aware of a problem.

Avoid a contingency that the buyer must be approved for a mortgage loan; the buyers should have been "qualified" by the real estate agent or "preapproved" by a lender. If you must agree to a clause about the buyer getting a mortgage approved, specify a deadline, a relatively short deadline.

A contingency that the buyers have to sell their home to buy your house is best avoided, but can be good or bad. If the buyers really, really want your house, they will drop the price of their house in order to sell—if they get an offer. If the buyers change their minds and do not want to go through with the deal and fulfill the P and S contract, the buyers just don't negotiate and agree on any offers to sell their house.

**Prior to Closing**

Expect the buyers to do a final walk through the day before closing, making sure any necessary and agreed upon repairs were made and seeing that everything else looks good (no holes in the wall or broken windows). Also, well in advance, notify the utility companies so the meters for the electricity and gas, if applicable, are read the day before closing, the town or city for the water meter reading, the telephone company so service is disconnected/changed, the post office so mail forwarded, and the cable television company so service is discontinued/changed on closing day; assuming you move out and the buyers move in that day. Make a checklist of things to do before closing.

## The Closing

Bring a pen, you use it frequently during the closing, after reading the documents, of course. The real estate agent should have addressed and resolved any problems or disagreements prior to closing. Therefore, the closing is hectic, but smooth.

At the conclusion, the buyers give you many, many thousands of dollars for a couple of keys.

## Summary

Get the most money for your house in the shortest period of time: market the house at the right price; do the necessary minor remodeling, repairs, and maintenance; do the right major remodeling, if any; focus on presentation and impression—every single day the house is on the market; and negotiate the selling price realistically.

# Chapter 11

# Save Money Buying a House

The two primary financial objectives when buying a house are pay as little for the house as reasonably possible and protect yourself from costly, aggravating problems and "misunderstandings." You have many tactics to achieve these objectives. The most important tactic when buying a house: get everything in writing. There are numerous steps between the statements "Let's buy a house" and "We own a new home!"

**Real Estate Agents**

Remember, the traditional real estate agent (and agency) represents the seller: legally and financially. The sales commission, usually a certain percentage of the selling price, is paid by the seller to the listing agency (and agent). The agent either finds a buyer, sells the house directly, and keeps the entire fee, or shares the fee with an another agent, who finds a buyer. Although typical agents represent the seller, the agents are usually responsible, fair, ethical, and honest in working with the buyer.

If you are selling your house and buying a house in the same area, you may want to work with one realtor. The agent should be more motivated to accomplish each task when one depends on the other. In addition, you are in a better position to negotiate the agent's commission for selling your property. Of course, if you are looking for a house in an entirely different area you need different agents.

The buyer agent, a person who represents the buyer legally and financially, is a relatively new development. I have not used a buyer agent. Exclusive buyer agents are independent, not affiliated with any real estate agency. Nonexclusive buyer agents are affiliated with an agency, which may or may not (preferably) be the agency selling the house you're buying. I have read that buyer agents may save their clients thousands of dollars in negotiating the selling price. Also, buyer agents do things seller agents usually do not do, such as cold calls and assist with buying for-sale-by-owner properties, as well as traditional services.

If you purchase a new house or one to be built, you may or may not deal with a real estate agent. Instead you may work directly with the builder or a representative of the builder.

Whether you work with an agent or a builder, you need to feel comfortable with and trust the individual. If a person is misleading, deceptive, or lies once, he or she can do it again. If you have any specific reason not to trust the agent, change the agent and agency.

**Before You Look at Your First House**

Before you pull up to the curb to seriously consider your first prospective house, answer several important questions. Addressing these questions in advance saves frustration, aggravation, and disappointment.

The most important question: What price range can you afford—realistically—and still sleep at night? Presumably you have a certain amount of money for a down payment. You don't want prices so high you can only afford the minimal down payment of, for example, five percent. Preferably, the price range allows a down payment of twenty percent to thirty-three percent, at least.

The answer to the first question impacts the second question: What town (or city) or part of a town, do you want to—can you realistically afford to—live in?  Location, location, location. Do your homework (small pun). Check the real estate section of the Sunday Newspaper to see about the type of houses and price ranges. If you can be restrained and unemotional during the homework phase: drive around; look at several homes, lots, and the prices—from your car. Has a house been on the market for a long time? Yes? That could be a sign of trouble for the house or neighborhood, or an opportunity for a bargain. You can ask a real estate agent how long a house has been available. Consider the neighborhood, distance and type of traffic to commute to work, school system, supermarkets and other stores, weather variables (e.g., near the ocean), and property taxes (if applicable).

Question three: Do you want a new house or an existing house? Each has advantages and disadvantages. A new house provides modern amenities, such as good insulation, new appliances, carpeting, plumbing, electrical wiring, windows, siding, and roof. Some amenities may cost you extra to upgrade. But you should not have to pay to repair or replace anything for a few years. If a problem develops, the builder or manufacturer's warranty should cover the expense. Everything is brand new, inside and outside. New and sparse landscaping: a great opportunity to create your own glorious world or a lot of work and money planting trees, flowers, and shrubs, and getting a lush lawn established.

An existing house may have wonderful landscaping, but the interior may not match your taste. You may want to or need to replace carpeting, drapes, and appliances, or modernize plumbing and electrical wiring, which could be expensive. However, a fix-it-up house could be in your price range and a bargain for a handy do-it-yourselfer. If the house is well maintained and nicely decorated you just move in, relax, and enjoy your comfortable new home.

Think about what features are essential for your home. Features include: amount of living space (square feet), three bedrooms or four bedrooms, big family room, kitchen with dining area, formal dining room, two-car garage, large lot, and walk-out basement. You probably can't have everything you want; so prioritize. What do you need for the present and future? Anticipate family needs and resale value too.

Fourth question: What about resale? It may seem strange to consider resale before you buy, but resale is crucial. A house is first a home, then an investment. A big investment. Sooner or later you will probably move. Your property should increase in value and be highly marketable. In ten years the inside of the house could look like Buckingham Palace, but sitting on a swampy, quarter-acre lot; who will buy the palace? It's difficult to increase the size of the lot. Twelve-room house—great; each room the size of a closet. Again, who will buy and, if somebody buys, how much will they pay? A

beautiful house, on a spacious, level lot, and from the living room—
a panoramic view of the nearby high-tension wires and towers.
How will the neighborhood (especially view and upkeep of property), noise (as a 747 flew over the pilot waved to you), ease of
commuting, and other factors related to location affect the future
value of your house? What can you change and not change inside
and outside the house? Be objective, think about resale. You are
naturally emotional over the features you need and love, and may
overlook the drawbacks, the negatives. Recognizing the negatives
before you buy makes a difference in thousands of future dollars.

To review, the questions to ask yourself before you seriously
consider your first house:
What price range can you afford—realistically—and still sleep at
night?
What town (or city) or part of a town, do you want to—can you
realistically afford to—live in?
Do you want a new house or an existing house?
What about resale?

Your answers to these questions will allow you to enjoy your
new home and save you tens of thousands of dollars: your mortgage will be realistic and manageable, you will win the mortgage
war easier and sooner, and you will have 100 percent equity on a
higher-valued property to put towards the purchase of your next
home (if desired).

### Selecting Your New Home

This is a short section. Based on the answers to the above questions
and your personal needs and wants, selecting your home is up to
you. Please be objective as well as subjective.

### Negotiating the Purchase Price

You found your dream house; now it's time to negotiate the purchase price. Your objective as the buyer is to pay as little for the
house as reasonably possible. Unfortunately, like the fountain of
youth, the single, universal, successful approach to buying does not
exist. There are many variables to weigh in negotiating.

One variable is the current real estate market specifically in the town and neighborhood. Disregard the town's real estate tax assessment value (which can be old and skewed by tax rates) and what the seller originally paid for the house. You need reliable, up-to-date information—on similar houses—about the selling prices, the differences between the asking and selling prices, and the length of time "your house" and others were on the market, as well as similar houses currently on the market and their asking prices. All this information is available through your real estate agent, or public documents for selling prices. Objectively based on selling price and time on the market, is "your house" overpriced, priced about right, or underpriced. Therefore, objectively, could/should your offer be substantially lower than the asking price, somewhat lower than the asking price, or near the asking price (you are getting a bargain).

Are other buyers interested in "your house"? If the house has been on the market for several months be skeptical if someone tells you two other buyers are also interested. If houses are on the market an average of two weeks in the neighborhood and the one you love was just listed last week, others may really be interested. You may need to be more generous in your offer than you anticipated; but not necessarily pay more for the house than its worth based on the market information.

Are you equally interested in other houses, in case this one does not work out? If so, you probably do not have to be generous in offering and negotiating a price.

If the house is a fix-it-upper, estimate how much you will have spend to improve the property and consider that amount in determining your offering price. If the house is perfect and you will not need to spend a dime, you have more room to negotiate.

If possible, learn about the sellers and why they are selling the house. Kids moved out, retirement to smaller home, job change, divorce, won the lottery: all influence the seller's motivation to negotiate and sell or not to sell. If the seller won the lottery either they can afford to sell for much less than the asking price, or they can afford to wait until he gets close to the asking price. Learn about the personalities of the seller. Would they respond favorably to the offer if you presented the objective information you based the offer on?  Perhaps if your agent presented the offer or counteroffer in person, at their home, the sellers would respond favorably. If the house has been on the market several months simply because the seller has refused several offers, be patient and observant. The price may plummet and the willingness to sell may soar next week.

The intangibles may be the most important variables. Buying and selling a house are emotional experiences for the buyer and seller. Both parties want to feel good about the outcome of the negotiation; perhaps feeling that they each got a "good price."

As the buyer, in negotiating, you should not only consider the current real estate market and the seller to negotiate, but also what the house is worth to you. You can say:  We agreed on a fair price and the house is worth it.  Or you can say:  The seller wanted more than I wanted to offer, and it was not worth it to me.  Or you can say:  Yes, I paid a little more than I wanted, but it is worth it to me. I'll take care of the property and it will increase in value to make up for the extra I paid.  When you agree on a price and you buy the house, the appropriate reaction is jubilation and excitement, not sadness and regret.  Negotiating with your brain and heart assures the appropriate reaction.

### The Deposit or Earnest Money

When you and the seller agree on an offer, you write a check as a deposit or earnest money, a way to demonstrate you're sincere and committed to buy the house. On the check write "deposit for purchase of house at [property address] for $XXX,XXX." This deposit and the purchase and sale agreement (P and S) are presented to the seller. Get a detailed receipt for the deposit.

Crucial:  Make sure—in writing—that the check will be deposited in an escrow account until the closing and the deposit is refundable if you fulfill the terms of the purchase and sale agreement, but the seller can not. The escrow account protects your money. Remember, it's still your money until you get something for it at closing, the house.

An escrow account is especially important for a house to be built—by a date specified in writing.  If the house is not built, you deserve to get your money back, rather than spent by the builder.

The builder may say he needs the deposit to start the house. Baloney. No escrow account, no deal.

My first house was supposed to be built, completed, ready to close, and move in on February 1st. On January 1st, I stood on the property with a newspaper from that day and took a photograph, proving that nothing had started (despite many weeks of the builder saying we'll begin soon). With persistence, a P and S specifying the closing date, a photograph, and, despite the builder's objections, my deposit in an escrow account: I got my money back.

Protect yourself and your deposit, insist on an escrow account. Don't give in (Well, . . . OK). Don't allow the builder or seller access to your money. Earnest money in escrow only.

## The Purchase and Sale Agreement

You have a deal; the next step is for you and the seller to sign the purchase and sale agreement (P and S). This is the sales contract, a binding legal document. Read it before signing. If you're the least bit uncomfortable, have your lawyer read the P and S before you sign.

You get a copy of the P and S for your records and to present to a lender when applying for a mortgage. Be sure you "qualify," not necessarily have approval, for a loan, before you sign the P and S, as you may not get your deposit back if you can not obtain a loan. The real estate agent should determine that you financially qualify to buy the property before you walk into the house. Sometimes you may want a lender to "pre-qualify" you. This means you choose a bank before you look for a house and they determine how much you can borrow (subject to approving the house as collateral).

Typically, the lender wants to know what property you are buying and what you are using as collateral (the specific house) before they give you a loan. (See Chapter 12)  If the purchase price is more than the house is worth, the lender may not give you a mortgage based on bank's appraisal of the property; the house is not sufficient collateral for the loan. And you may not get your deposit back.

## Home Inspection

For an existing house, especially an old house, make sure the P and S contains a "contingency" that the house is subject to a professional home inspection. It costs you a few hundred dollars, but a home inspection can save you a few thousand dollars and bad headaches.

Depending on the results of the inspection you have: peace of mind (and legal recourse against the inspector, if he missed a significant defect), grounds for an adjustment of the selling price of the house (to repair an undisclosed or unknown, significant defect), or grounds for a refund of your deposit (undisclosed or unknown, colossal defect found). The inspection also is good for the seller; if there are no defects you have no legitimate reason to back out of the deal.

Find a reliable home inspector. Your real estate agent can recommend one, but there may be a conflict of interest. The inspector may not get referrals if he finds too many things wrong with the house. Be skeptical if the inspector is part of a contractor company, what a nice way to get repair business. Get references and check them thoroughly. Call the Better Business Bureau and state licensing agency (if applicable). Make sure—verify—that the inspector has liability insurance. If he misses a major defect, the liability insurance should cover the cost of repairs. Ask if he has a warranty for the inspection results.

Accompany the inspector when he or she is inspecting. This is expected, not an insult. Your real estate agent usually joins in too. You see that the inspection is complete, observe any problems, get some helpful hints about maintaining the house, and receive the verbal report. You can even videotape the inspection, which may help if a serious problem is missed. A written report will follow, documenting that a checklist of items were satisfactory or unsatisfactory, in addition to a summary statement about his findings.

Actually, perform a personal, informal, nonprofessional home inspection before you negotiate. Your inspection consists of asking and checking. Even though your real estate agent should disclose any problems with the property: question, question, question. For example, ask about: plumbing problems (such as leaks, noise, and low water pressure), heating/cooling problems (inefficient system [the cost to heat the house for the winter/cool for the summer]), electrical problems (amp service for the house, blown fuses/tripped circuit breaker), problems with insects (termites, carpenter ants, others), water in the basement (in certain areas it may be expected), and the age of the roof.

In addition to asking, check carefully. Subjectively you love the house, but it's best to objectively look for problems now, before you buy the house. Try to open a few windows. If one or two get stuck or a sash cord is broken, try some more. Check the floors, the ones without carpeting. Are they nearly level? No floor is perfectly level, but a marble should not accelerate toward a wall. Check for cracks in the walls, floor tiles, ceilings, and foundation. Look under the kitchen and bathroom sinks. Are there signs of leaks or insects, dead or alive? Turn on the burners and oven of the stove. Try the garbage disposal. The personal home inspection (accompanied by your agent, of course) works best when the homeowner is not home.

If you find a defect requiring repair, make sure the P and S includes a contingency clause stating that either the defect will be repaired and approved by you prior to closing, or the selling price will be reduced by the amount necessary to make the repairs.

The personal and professional home inspections help assure peace of mind. If problems are identified, either you do not buy the house, or you buy the house knowing that certain repairs are needed, sooner or later.

**Second Thoughts**

The P and S is signed, the first reaction is yippee, and the second reaction may be oh-oh, did I do the right thing? Excitement followed by anxiety, especially for first-time buyers. Second- and third-timers can worry, too; they also have to sell a house. Buying a house means a mortgage process which may be intimidating, a gigantic commitment and, substantial debt. Apprehension is natural.

Overcome the anxiety by focusing on and talking about the reason for the excitement—the marvelous house and your plans for the house (e.g., new flowers or great family room). Become familiar and comfortable with the process of obtaining a mortgage. Remember, the lender makes money by loaning you money. The bank wants your business (assuming you have good credit). This is also a good time to reinforce you commitment to pay off your mortgage and win the mortgage war as soon as possible; thus eliminating the debt and increasing the excitement. Finally, maintain your perspective and priorities: buying a house and getting a mortgage is not a matter of life and death.

**Prior to Closing**

The day before closing, walk through the house to see that it still looks the same as when you signed the P and S. No damage. Nothing is removed, like the chandelier; unless agreed to and stated in the P and S. Make sure any contingencies are met satisfactorily.

Arrange for telephone and cable television service to begin, the electricity and gas meters to be read, and mail delivery to start on closing day; if you're moving in to your new house that day. Of course, also stop these services at your soon-to-be old house.

**The Closing**

The closing can be hectic, with lots of papers to read and sign, but there should be no surprises. Take your time. Resolve any problems, disagreements, or contingencies prior to closing. The real estate agent helps assure a smooth process between the P and S signing and the closing.

**Summary**

First, ask yourself the four big questions:

What price range can you afford—realistically—and still sleep at night?

What town (or city) or part of a town, do you want to—can you realistically afford to—live in?

Do you want a new house or an existing house?

What about resale?

Then find your dream house and negotiate the price based on up-to-date, objective information on the real estate market in your area. If possible, learn about the sellers and why they're selling. This information can influence the amount of the offer and the way the offer is made. Always consider what the house is worth to you. The less you pay for your house, the smaller the mortgage.

Get everything in writing. Receipt for the earnest money, purchase and sale agreement stating that the deposit is to be held in escrow and is refundable if the seller does not meet the terms of the contract, home inspection report—all in writing. Avoid costly misunderstandings, problems, and the aggravation of filing a lawsuit.

Next, live happily ever after in your new home.

# Chapter 12

# Get the Best Mortgage

This chapter discusses many tactics to save the most money when you obtain the loan for the largest purchase of your life. Getting a mortgage can be a perplexing and costly process, especially for first-timers.

Doing your mortgage homework eases the process and pays off in thousands of dollars saved, even before extra to principal (ETP) payments. Use available resources and be open-minded, don't restrict yourself to the bank where you have a checking and savings account.

## Getting Started

Look in the Sunday newspaper real estate section for a table prepared by a state banking or similar agency which lists financial institutions and their mortgage interest rates. The table may list the lenders, the fifteen-year rate, the thirty-year rate, the variable rate, and the down payment percentage required. The lenders also have other loans and rates available.

The lender does not have to have an office in the town or city you are living in or are moving to. The institution just has to provide loans for buying property in your future hometown. Consider credit unions, they are usually extremely competitive, but they may not appear on the state banking list.

The lender must be reliable. It's important your loan be processed correctly and efficiently. You don't want to be sitting at the closing wondering why the lender's check is not ready. Ask your real estate agent for the names of dependable lenders and about lenders you found in your research. Call the state banking agency and the Better Business Bureau to see if complaints are on file against lenders you're considering. Narrow the field; say to five to ten lenders. Telephone them to get more information.

The information allows you to accurately budget for expenses, comparison shop, and negotiate. In a competitive market, a preferred lender may match another lender's closing costs. It never hurts to ask, especially if you make a large down payment and have an excellent credit record; both of which mean reduced risk for the bank. You may lower your closing costs by several hundred dollars.

## Closing Costs or Settlement Charges

The closing costs or settlement charges include several expenses related to getting a mortgage that vary by state and financial institution. Prepare a chart to document everything you discuss on the telephone: the estimated closing costs or settlement charges, the current interest rates on the loans (e.g., fifteen-year and thirty-year) you are interested in, when the rates are subject to change, and the "points" if any. Always document the name of the person you speak with and the date and time of the discussion.

### Mortgage Application Fee

The mortgage application fee pays for the privilege of applying for a loan. This fee is usually not refundable, but ask anyway.

### Title Charges

Title charges include the bank's attorney's fee, the municipal lien certificate, and the bank's title insurance coverage. You pay for the bank's attorney to represent the bank's interest. Of course, you also need to pay an attorney to represent your interests.

The municipal lien certificate documents that there are no (apparent) liens, such as another mortgage, on the property or title.

The title is the evidence that gives rise to a legal right of possession of the property. Title insurance protects the bank's investment (the amount of the loan) and property value against loss because of an error in the title to the property, a lien on the title, and other problems related to the title. You may also want to have title insurance to protect you (for the full value of your property). If you and the lender purchase your individual title insurance policies from the same title insurance company at the same time, the cost for your coverage is usually lower than if you bought your insurance independently.

Government Recording Charges

Government recording charges include the recording fees for the deed and the mortgage, which covers the paperwork and the legwork. The deed is the document that legally transfers the title, with the right of ownership, from the seller to the buyer.

Payment in Advance to the Lender

Payment in advance to the lender includes prepaid interest (interest on the loan from the closing date until the payment due date), mortgage insurance premium (if applicable), and hazard insurance premium (if applicable). Mortgage insurance is usually required if the amount of the loan is greater than a certain percentage (e.g., eighty percent) of the appraised value of the property. This is the lender's insurance. Mortgage insurance guarantees that the loan is repaid if you are unable to pay the mortgage. (You can purchase mortgage life insurance for yourself. Mortgage life insurance pays off the mortgage if you die. However, you may prefer the beneficiary be responsible for handling the mortgage.) If you do not pay the lender for hazard insurance, you probably have to obtain home owner's insurance before the closing. Of course, you want adequate home owner's insurance anyway.

Items Payable in Connection with the Loan

Items payable in connection with the loan include the appraisal fee, the credit report fee, and the loan origination fee ("points"). The appraisal fee covers the costs of an independent appraiser documenting that the property you are purchasing is worth the price you're paying and the price the bank is using to determine the collateral for the loan. The appraised value and the amount of your down payment dictate if you are required to have mortgage insurance.

The credit report fee covers the cost of obtaining your credit history from a credit bureau. Have you paid your bills and paid them on time? There can be errors in credit histories and you have the right to dispute inaccurate information. If you had a credit problem, volunteer the information to the lender when you apply for the loan, explain the circumstances, describe how the problem was resolved, and provide documentation. When you win the mortgage war with many large ETP payments, you have an excellent credit rating.

Loan origination fee or "points"

The loan origination fee or "points" is a percentage of the loan amount that's paid in advance. One point on a $100,000 loan is one percent of $100,000 or $1,000 paid at closing. Two points on a $75,000 loan is $1,500. Lenders say the fee or points covers the cost of processing the loan and eventually selling the loan on the secondary market.

Points may also be considered prepayment of interest. The points range from zero to five percent of the loan amount. In general, when you pay points the interest rate on the loan is less than with no points. Determine if you save more money with a somewhat higher interest rate and higher monthly payments, but no points. How long will it take—without ETP payments—to break-even?

For example, how does a thirty-year, $100,000 mortgage at 8 percent interest compare with a thirty-year, $100,000 mortgage at 7.75 percent interest and two points? The monthly payments are $733.77 and $716.42 for the 8 percent rate and the 7.75 percent rate, respectively. The savings is $17.35 a month with the 7.75 percent rate and two points. But the two points cost you $2,000 (two percent of $100,000) in advance. Therefore, the 7.75 percent interest and two points takes 115 months, about ten years, to break-even with the 8 percent interest. In this case, you are probably better off paying the slightly higher interest rate and no points.

Points usually may be deducted as interest on your federal income tax in the year the points were paid. Depending on your tax bracket, the $2,000 paid in points and used as a deduction saves you about $300 to $720 in federal income tax. Therefore, the net cost of the points is $1,700 to $1,280. And the after-tax-deduction break-even point is ninety-eight months (eight years) to seventy-four months (six years), respectively.

In this example, you are definitely better off when you make large ETP payments and win the mortgage war in less than six years (or you move within six years).

Points paid on refinancing a mortgage are usually only deductible by dividing the amount paid over the term of the mortgage. For the above example, $2,000 in points divided by thirty (thirty-year loan) equals a deduction of a stupendous $66.67. Depending on your tax bracket, the $66.67 deduction saves you just $10 to $24 a year. And if you move before thirty years, the points deduction is gone. Remember, tax laws can change.

Additional Settlement Charges

Additional settlement charges may include survey or plot plan, document preparation fee, and express mailing. The survey or plot plan is typically a simple diagram of the lot and structures on the land, based on tape measurements. It's usually not an instrument survey with boundary markers. The plot plan also documents that the property is or is not in a flood zone, is properly zoned (i.e., residential), and does or does not have any easements. An easement is a right of way on the property, such as for a utility company.

## Negotiate

Use negotiation as a money-saving tactic, especially from strength. When you find a reliable lender, ask your preferred lender to waive some closing costs or match the closing costs of lower-priced competitors. Your preferred lender is more receptive when you make a large down payment and have an excellent credit rating.

Also, consider asking the sellers of the house you are buying to share or cover your closing costs as part of the purchase and sale agreement. The longer the house has been on the market, the more agreeable the sellers.

## Fixed Rate Mortgage or Adjustable Rate Mortgage

Generally, you choose between a mortgage with an interest rate that is constant for the life of the loan, a fixed rate mortgage (FRM), or a mortgage with an interest rate lower than a FRM initially, but adjusted up or down after a certain period of time, an adjustable rate mortgage (ARM). The lower initial interest rate of the ARM may last for one year up to four or five years. Initial interest rates guaranteed for one year are usually less than rates secured for four or five years. Of course, the lower rates are subject to increase after only one year.

After the initial guaranteed period, the rate may increase or decrease depending on a specified financial index, such as one-year Treasury issues, three-year Treasury issues, or five-year Treasury issues. There is a limit to how much the interest rate can increase for any period (commonly one year). The yearly limit is usually a one percent or two percent increase. There is also a limit to how much the interest rate can increase over the life of the loan, usually a maximum of six percent increase above the initial rate. The rate may also decrease, but there may be a minimum rate.

I recommend a FRM, especially for your first mortgage and if you have trouble sleeping. True, the interest rate is typically higher for the FRM than the ARM, but you will be aggressively paying ETP; so the actual interest dollars paid will be drastically reduced. Also, with the FRM, if the interest rates decrease you can refinance to a lower fixed rate.

For your second house consider an ARM. When you use your 100 percent equity from your first mortgage victory you have a smaller loan for the second house. Also, you are accustomed to making aggressive ETP payments. An ARM, with the initial lower interest rate on a smaller loan, leaves you more money for even larger ETP payments.

## Fifteen-Year Mortgage or Thirty-Year Mortgage

The two most common mortgage terms are fifteen years and thirty years. The interest rate on a fifteen-year mortgage is usually less than a thirty-year mortgage, about one-quarter percent less. And there's a big difference in the total interest dollars you pay over the term of the loan.

I recommend a fifteen-year mortgage because the shorter life saves interest dollars. The classic example is the $100,000 loan at ten percent interest. For the fifteen-year mortgage you pay approximately $200,000 over the life of the loan, $100,000 in principal and $100,000 in interest. For the thirty-year mortgage you pay approximately $300,000 over the life of the loan, $100,000 in principal and $200,000 in interest. When you double the life of the loan, you approximately double the interest you pay, with the same amount of principal repaid, of course. The fifteen-year mortgage has somewhat higher basic monthly payments (about twenty percent to thirty percent higher), but you save interest dollars even before ETP payments. If you're not able to continue the mortgage war, you still save interest with the fifteen-year loan over the thirty-year loan. A ten-year mortgage saves even more interest.

## No Prepayment Penalty

It is crucial—be absolutely sure—there is a statement in the mortgage contract that documents there is "no prepayment penalty." When you make ETP payments you are making prepayments. The statement "no prepayment penalty" guarantees you do not have to pay extra, a penalty, because you sacrificed and made ETP payments.

Prepayment penalties are relatively rare and illegal in certain states. Originally, when many lenders had no points, prepayment penalties discouraged borrowers from switching banks when the rates decreased. With points, changing banks is less economical and less likely. Also, prepayment penalties intended to prevent a borrower from refinancing a loan with another lender may not be enforced when you pay off the loan with ETP payments. But why take a chance; get it in writing: "no prepayment penalty."

Many loans are purchased on the secondary mortgage market and some buyers forbid prepayment penalties. Certain mortgage purchasers, such as the Federal National Mortgage Association (Fannie Mae), the Federal Home Loan Mortgage Corporation (Freddie Mac), and the Government National Mortgage Association (Gennie Mac), do not buy loans with prepayment penalties.

## Overkill in Applying

Take everything you have related to your finances to the lender when applying for a mortgage. This includes assets and income: checkbook, most recent checking account and savings account statements, photocopies of stocks, bonds, mutual funds statements or other assets, most recent pay stubs, and proof of any other income. Also, take information on any liabilities: most recent credit card statement(s), car loan payments, proof of rent or mortgage payments. You smile when you present statements showing no credit card balance, the car loan discharge (paid off many months ahead of schedule) and the title to the car, and a mortgage discharge (paid off many years ahead of schedule) and the title for your current house.

Favorably impress the loan officer, save time and aggravation, and get your loan application approved with your well-organized financial documents.

## Document, Document, Document

Get everything in writing. Take notes during any telephone conversations or discussions in person. Include the names of individuals, and the dates and times of discussions. Read all documents carefully before signing anything. Although usually unnecessary when working with a reputable lender, consider having your lawyer review documents before signing, if you're uncomfortable. Get and keep a copy of all signed documents. Maintain organized files for all notes and documents. You maintain control of the process and have some peace of mind when you protect yourself from unanticipated expenses and aggravation by documenting everything and being organized. Do not assume anything; get everything in writing.

## Summary

Many tactics make getting a mortgage relatively easy and save money. The information you obtain from several lenders allows you to compare interest rates and closing costs, shop around, and get the best mortgage with the lowest closing costs from a reliable lender.

For your first mortgage, I recommend a fifteen-year, fixed-rate mortgage with no points. After you have won a mortgage war, consider a fifteen-year, adjustable-rate mortgage with no points. You save thousands of dollars.

Chapter 13

# How to Make Extra to Principal Payments—Step by Step

After "I love you," my favorite words in the English language are "extra to principal." For you, writing this phrase on a check every month is enjoyment. The greater the number of dollars written with the phrase, the greater the enjoyment.

Big extra to principal (ETP) payments are the positive reinforcement and big reward for your determination, mortgage goal, spend-less-money mindset, and sacrifices; you have the money to aggressively reduce the mortgage.

**Do It Yourself**

There is absolutely, positively no need to have a bank, an agency, or a service make special arrangements—with (especially) or without a fee—for your ETP payments. Making ETP payments is easy and strictly do-it-yourself.

It's important that the bank properly credit your ETP payments. You want to avoid any chance of error or fraud. The error may occur if the ETP money is applied to the wrong category, such as to interest or to the escrow account for taxes (if required for your mortgage).

Fraud is always possible if you give your money to a service to pay the bank. The agency could pay the bank the basic principal and interest, and keep your ETP money. The bank would receive the expected basic principal and interest payments and would not send you overdue notices. Months later you learn that the agency pocketed your ETP payments. A postcard from the Bahamas may be your first indication of a problem. Also, the agency could keep the entire amount and you would miss one or more mortgage payments.

You would lose all your money and risk having missed mortgage payments on your credit history. Perhaps you could avoid the latter by working with the bank, considering the fraud (if you had proof). You are legally responsible; be personally responsible.

## Making ETP Payments

You probably make your mortgage payment based on either a monthly bill and statement or a coupon book. Remember, the goal is for the bank to correctly process the ETP payment. It's easier to avoid problems than to resolve them.

### Bill and Statement

If you receive a bill and statement each month, identify the box for "extra to principal" on the part of the bill that is returned to the bank. In red ink, write the ETP portion of the total amount in the "extra to principal" box. Circle that area and draw an arrow to it, in red ink. You want someone who is handling hundreds of these documents in a month to notice your important difference. Do not use a felt-tipped marker, because it can smudge. And do not use a pencil, because it can be erased and changed.

Use one personal check to pay the total amount: basic principal (P), interest (I), taxes (T) to escrow [if applicable], home owner's insurance (IS) [if applicable], and your ETP payment each month. Use a personal check so you get the canceled check back each month. On the face of the check, write in the total amount, the loan or account number, and the due date in black or blue ink. Black ink makes a better photocopy than blue ink, if a copy is ever needed. If your name and address are preprinted on the check, write a large FOR next to that information. If your name address are not on the check, print them on the check. Print "Extra to Principal $X,XXX" in red ink prominently on the face of the check and circle it. Try to round off ETP amounts to whole hundred dollars (e.g., $400, $700,

$1,100). It may seem like a lot of information for each check, but it's worth it to avoid problems. After you've done it a couple of times, the whole process takes less than five minutes.

Save all canceled checks permanently, especially all your mortgage payments. In your checkbook, document the amount of ETP payment and the amount to P/I/(T/IS) with each entry. On the portion of the bank statement you keep for your records (permanently), write the check number, the date, the total amount paid, and the amount paid ETP. In your notebook monthly record, document the total and ETP amounts.

You should follow this procedure whether you pay in person at the bank or by mail. If there's ever any problem, the more complete and organized your documentation, the better.

After your first ETP payment, check the statement each month to make sure the ETP is properly credited to your loan. There should be an area on the statement showing the portion of the basic payment that went to reduce the principal, the ETP payment that went to reduce the principal, and the new and improved (reduced) principal balance. Is this information correct?

Each month you are ecstatic to see the part of the basic payment that goes to principal progressively increase, the part of the basic payment that goes to interest progressively decrease, and best of all, the principal balance shrink towards zero.

Coupon Book

If you use a coupon book, the procedure for payments is similar to the bill and statement. Write in the ETP payment amount on the coupon as described above for the bill. Write out the check and document in the checkbook as above. Also, write in the information (total amount paid, check number and date) on the stub in the coupon book, plus the ETP and P/I(T/IS) payments.

The big difference between the coupon book and monthly statements and bills is that with the coupons you can not automatically confirm that the monthly ETP and other payments have been accurately processed. Therefore, if you pay in person, first have your payments (basic and ETP) applied to the loan and then request a summary statement for your account. If you pay by mail, each month, after the bank has had time to receive and process the payment, call the bank (preferably with an 800 number or a local call) and request that an account summary statement be mailed to you. Check the statement to be sure the ETP and other payments are right.

Confirm accuracy every month. If not checked every month, any error or embezzlement (eventually discovered) is extremely aggravating to correct. Since each month's basic principal and interest amounts depend on the previous month's principal reduction, all of the payments made after the month in which the error or errors occurred has to be adjusted. Save all the account summary statements, checks, and the coupon books.

The account summary statements give you supreme pleasure and positive reinforcement; confirming that with ETP payments you win a mortgage battle every month.

### Summary

Follow these payment procedures: document, document, document. Minimize or eliminate payment problems. You're well on your way to a happy end to your mortgage.

# Part V

# The War Begins

# Chapter 14

# The Conclusion and The Beginning

The opening sentence of the Introduction: "Imagine how you will feel free of debt; your home mortgage paid off many years or decades ahead of schedule." Now you know how to do more than just imagine the feeling—make it reality and enjoy the debt-free feeling. Win the mortgage war.

Establish your ultimate goal and mortgage goal, and focus on the big benefits of achieving those goals. Based on these personal goals, establish the right priorities and achieve the major objectives: reduce expenses and reduce spending.

Use the same tactics I used to win the mortgage war twice: manage your finite resources wisely (based on your goals and priorities), observe the Nine Commandments of Purchasing, save money with smart supermarket shopping, promote and maintain good health, and decrease expenses around the house. For every purchase, small to large—throughout every day—maintain the spend-less-money mindset. Even small steps, such as savings money and natural resources by not continuously running the water while brushing your teeth, make a difference. Think before doing. Make the spend-less-money mindset second nature.

The daily savings add up and up over the weeks, months, and years. To emphasize that point, I always remember a television commercial for an electric shaver for men. It went something like this: Some men look at shaving as something you do once a day. At (manufacturer's name), we look at shaving as something you do for a lifetime. Make saving money, reducing expenses, reducing spending, a mindset and a practice for a lifetime. The accumulated savings go directly to large extra to principal (ETP) payments each month and early mortgage victory, and the ultimate goal.

Also save money by using the tactics to get the best mortgage, and in buying a house. If you are selling your house, get the most money for it. When you win the mortgage war, the entire selling price (less sales commission) goes toward the down payment for the next house.

Use the step-by-step guidelines for making the ETP payments to assure your payments are credited properly. Watch and smile as the amount of basic interest drops, the amount of basic principal rises, and the principal balance plummets. You know every month your efforts and sacrifices are paying off in saving thousands of dollars of total interest and eliminating the mortgage and debt years ahead of schedule.

Slash the most years and the most interest dollars off your mortgage: make ETP payments as early in the term as possible, ideally the first month, and as large as possible. The charts and diagrams in Chapter 5, Finances 102 (page 29), let you see how quickly your ETP payments pay off the mortgage and how much interest you save, especially if you are just beginning to pay off your new mortgage. Refer to this information to help plan your strategy for mortgage victory, including the amount of your monthly ETP payments.

A winning philosophy, a winning attitude, is necessary for mortgage victory. The military leaders began Desert Storm with a winning attitude and we know the outcome of that war. You win the mortgage war with the same attitude. "I can, I can, I can," becomes a self-fulfilling prophecy.

It just makes sense to take control of your finances, eliminate debt, and achieve and enjoy your ultimate goal. I did it. I bought my second house—using the 100 percent equity from paying off the mortgage on my first house in just six years—and achieved a second mortgage victory in two years. You can do it too. You know the strategies and tactics necessary to win the mortgage war.

Begin the mortgage war today.

# Index

# Order Form

Please send _____ copy(ies) of:

*How to Win the Mortgage War—*
*No Mortgage, No Debt, In as Little as Two Years*

To:                              (please print)

Name _____

Address _____

City _____ State _____ Zip _____ - _____

Telephone ( _____ ) _____ - _____

Price:  $19.95 each

Sales Tax:
Please add $1 for each book shipped to Massachusetts addresses.

Shipping:
Please add $2 for one book, and $1 for each additional book.
(Allow three to four weeks for delivery.)

Mail Order Form and total amount in check or money order
(no C.O.D.s please) to:

Sirrom Publishing
Post Office Box 40
Marlborough, Massachusetts 01752-0040

Thank You

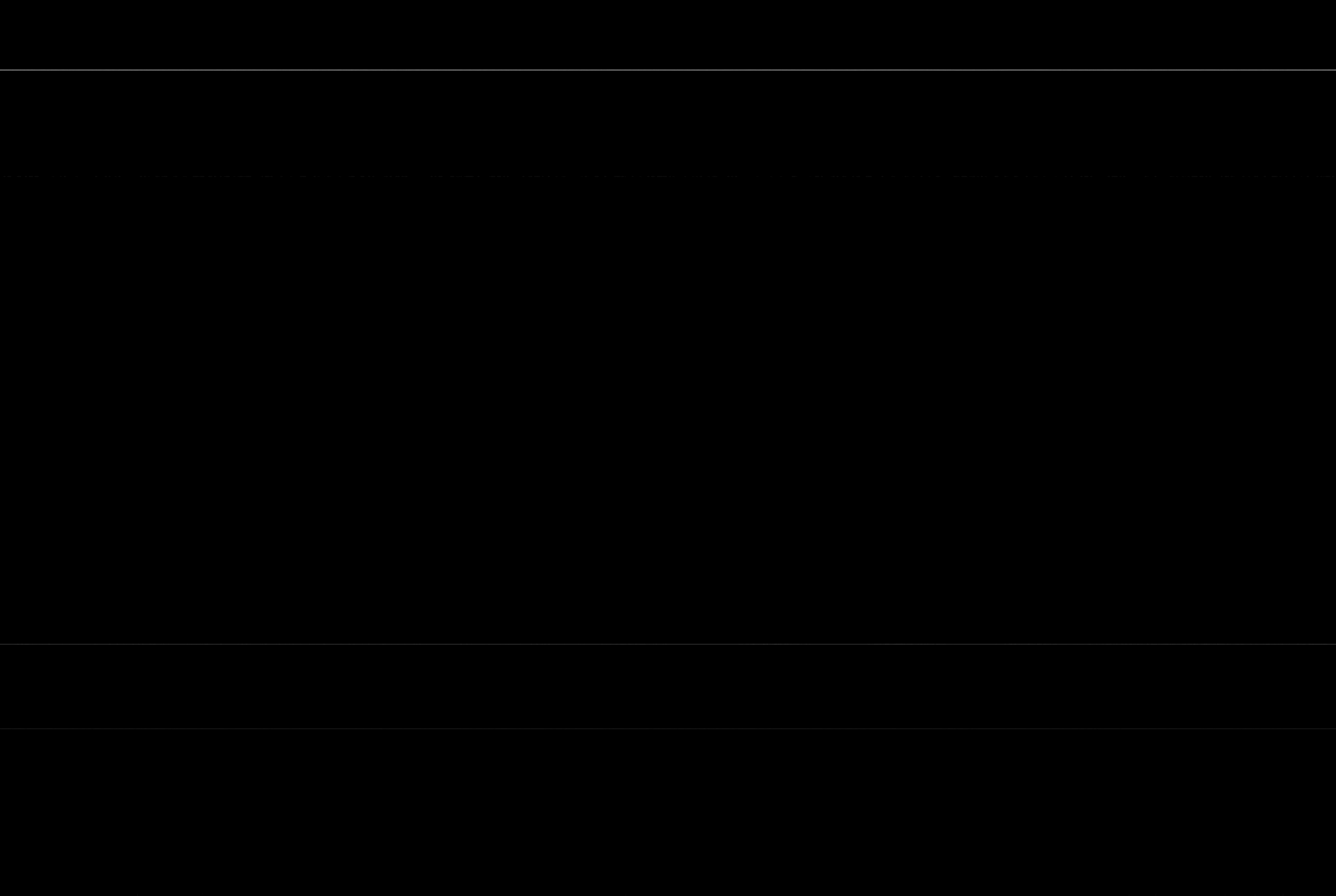

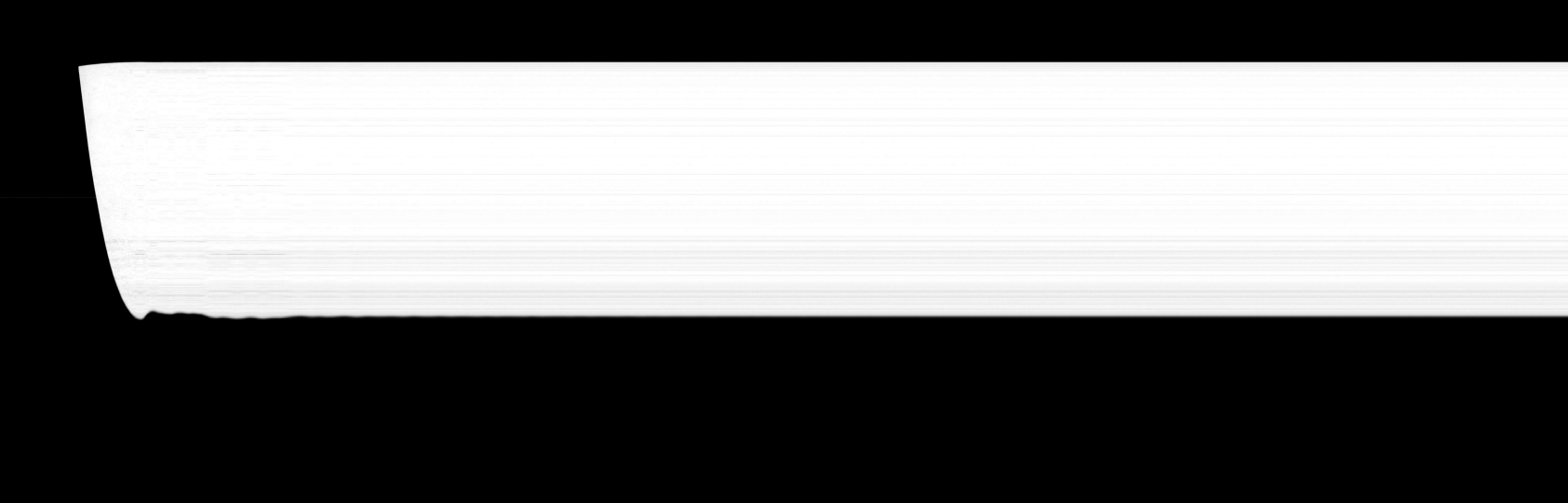

# Order Form

Please send _____ copy(ies) of:

*How to Win the Mortgage War—*
*No Mortgage, No Debt, In as Little as Two Years*

To:                          (please print)

Name _____

Address _____

City _____ State _____ Zip _____ - _____

Telephone ( _____ ) _____ - _____

Price:  $19.95 each

Sales Tax:
Please add $1 for each book shipped to Massachusetts addresses.

Shipping:
Please add $2 for one book, and $1 for each additional book.
(Allow three to four weeks for delivery.)

Mail Order Form and total amount in check or money order
(no C.O.D.s please) to:

Sirrom Publishing
Post Office Box 40
Marlborough, Massachusetts 01752-0040

Thank You